Walking the Castles of Kent

David Harrison

S.B. Publications

To my wife, Vivienne, without whose
help, patience and understanding,
none of this would have been possible.

First published in 2007 by S. B. Publications
Tel: 01323 893498
Email: sbpublications@tiscali.co.uk

ISBN 978-185770-327-6

Designed and Typeset by EH Graphics (01273) 515527

Front cover photos: *Sissinghurst, Deal, Cooling, Rochester and Scotney Castles.*
Back cover photo: *Hever Castle and topiary.*
Title page photo: *Cooling Castle.*

Walking the Castles of Kent

The walk is 193.4 miles (311.0km) long and starts at Richborough Castle. Setting out along the coast in a clockwise direction it visits 25 castles en route to Canterbury. In geographical order the castles visited are: Richborough - Sandown - Deal - Walmer - Dover - Castle Hill (Folkestone) - Saltwood - Lympne - Stutfall - Sissinghurst - Scotney - Castle Hill (Brenchley) - Tonbridge - Chiddingstone - Hever - Lullingstone - Eynsford - Cooling - Upnor - Rochester - Allington - Sutton Valence - Leeds - Chilham - Canterbury.

The route is split into 14 sections which do not necessarily represent a day's walking.

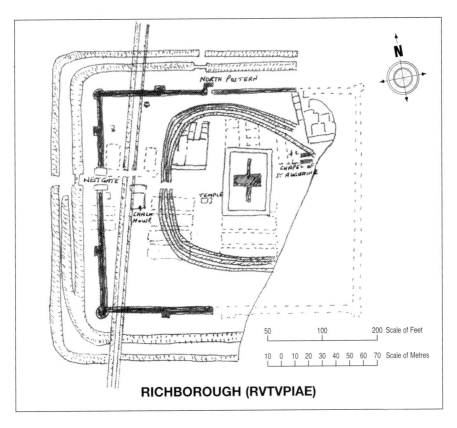

RICHBOROUGH (RVTVPIAE)

Richborough Castle, north wall and remains of buildings in north-east corner of site.

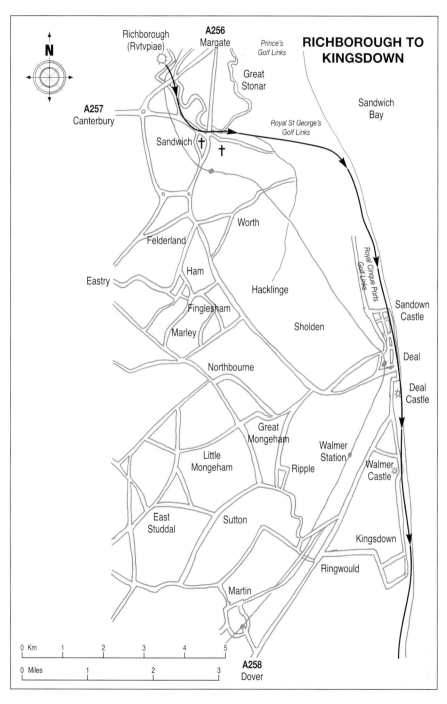

N

RICHBOROUGH TO KINGSDOWN

A256
Margate

Richborough
(Rvtvpiae)

Prince's
Golf Links

Great
Stonar

Sandwich
Bay

A257
Canterbury

Royal St George's
Golf Links

Sandwich

Worth

Felderland

Ham

Eastry

Hacklinge

Finglesham

Sholden

Royal Cinque Ports
Golf Links

Sandown
Castle

Marley

Deal

Northbourne

Deal
Castle

Great
Mongeham

Walmer
Station

Little
Mongeham

Walmer
Castle

Ripple

East
Studdal

Sutton

Kingsdown

Ringwould

Martin

| 0 Km | 1 | 2 | 3 | 4 | 5 |

| 0 Miles | 1 | 2 | 3 |

A258
Dover

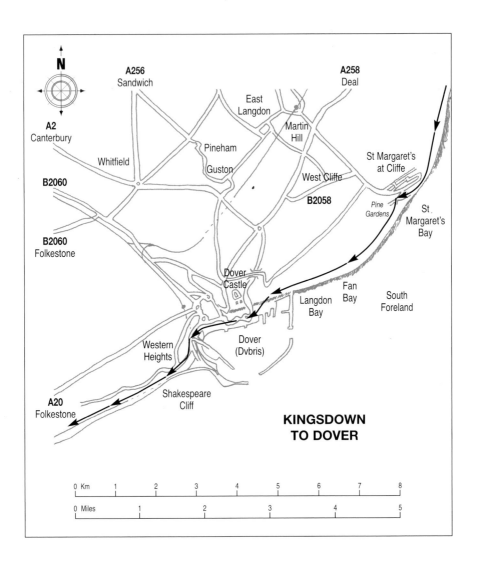

KINGSDOWN TO DOVER

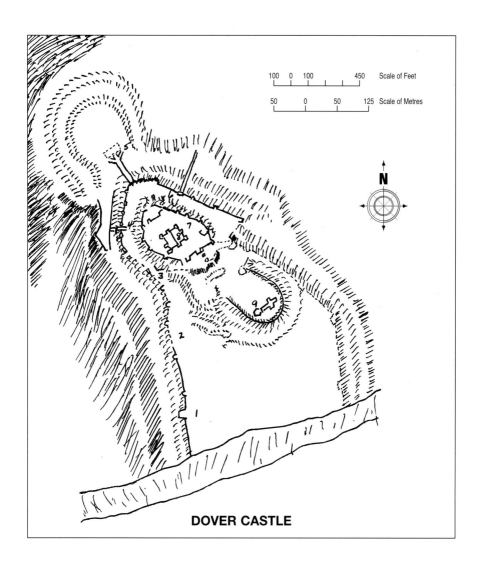

100 0 100   450 Scale of Feet

50   0   50   125 Scale of Metres

N

DOVER CASTLE

South Foreland lighthouse. Although no longer used as an aid to navigation it was used for Marconi's early broadcasts.

St. Margaret's Bay.

A Brief History of Castles

After the Norman Conquest in 1066, William the Conqueror rewarded the noblemen who fought for him by giving them large areas of land. Because of their fear of the Saxons, whose land they had possessed, and their distrust of each other, they sought a means of protecting themselves and opted for a fortified castle, generally on the highest ground of their estates.

Consisting of a solid, stone-built "keep", generally three or four floors high, and in the centre of a large courtyard enclosed by a strong and high stone wall up to ten feet thick, the castle was surrounded by a deep water-filled moat crossed by a drawbridge. Living quarters were usually on the first and second floors of the "keep" with the ground floor used for stores. The dungeon, below ground, was where captured enemies were imprisoned, sometimes for many years. The "keep" would have been a cold, draughty building, damp and uncomfortable, with unglazed slits for windows. Fires were built on the stone floor of the great hall, but without chimneys the room would soon become chokingly dense with smoke.

In more settled times, the lords built more spacious and comfortable living quarters within the castle walls so that the larger castles became more like small fortified towns. Bare stone walls were covered with huge tapestries, rugs were laid on the cold stone floors and furniture was made more comfortable, making the living quarters more gratifying. Come the Tudor period and more peaceful times, the castle gave way to country houses and palaces which were brighter and much more pleasant to live in.

Our discovery of Castles in Kent begins with the earliest visible traces of the Roman invasion of Britain: Rvtvpiae, or Richborough as we know it. The site lies one and a half miles (2.4km) north-west of Sandwich, along a minor road off the A257 to Canterbury.

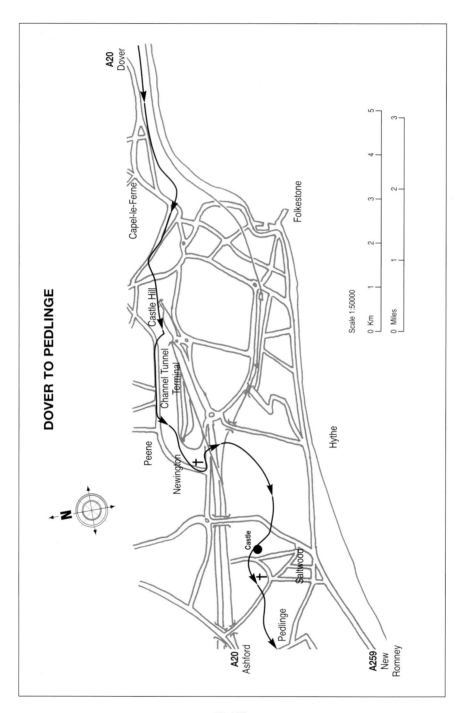

DOVER TO PEDLINGE

A20 Dover

Capel-le-Ferne

Castle Hill

Channel Tunnel Terminal

Peene

Newington

Folkestone

Hythe

Castle

Saltwood

Pedlinge

A20 Ashford

A259 New Romney

Scale 1:50000

0 Km 1 2 3 4 5

0 Miles 1 2 3

N

Richborough to Dover

RICHBOROUGH. Here was where the legions of Emperor Claudius arrived in AD43 during the main Roman invasion of England and the castle was constructed by the Romans in the third century as part of their protection against the Saxons. With walls 25 feet high and 11 feet wide over 1,000 feet still stand today 1700 years later. Great ditches were dug, 12 feet wide and 6 feet deep and 100 feet long, to defend themselves, and it was here the first stones of Watling Street were laid, the first road ever to be made in Britain.

Fragments of Early Iron Age pottery were found on the site, which would suggest occupation around the third century BC, but it was the four legions and auxiliaries under the command of Aulus Plautius that underlined its importance in history.

The site was most probably the Roman base until the success of the invasion was ensured, for the parallel defensive ditches date from around that period. By AD54 it became a supply depot and the buildings either side of these ditches were erected, north of the east-west road and near the entrance of the earlier camp. About the same time a series of granaries and other large buildings were erected on the other side of the east-west road.

Around AD85 all these wooden buildings were cleared away so that a splendid marble-cased building, decked with bronze statues, probably in honour of Emperor Domitian to commemorate the final conquest of Britain by Agricola, could be built. The foundation of this still exists today, 126 feet by 82 feet and over 30 feet thick, made up of layers of flint embedded in mortar.

By the second half of the third century came a fresh military occupation and an earth fort with the triple ditches was dug to protect the coast, probably from Saxon sea-rovers. Not long afterwards saw the construction of the great stone walls of the "Saxon Shore Fort", designed to protect the coast against Saxon raiders. The intensity of the fort's occupation is apparent by the discovery of thousands of coins belonging to the late fourth and early fifth centuries.

Guide to the Fortifications Facing the car park is the south wall of the Saxon Shore Fort with its two ditches. The east end of this wall and the whole of the east wall have disappeared, but the rest of the fortifications still stand, in places 25 feet high.

The main entrance is in the middle of the west wall and there presumably was a similar gate opposite on the east wall. In the middle of the north wall is a postern and traces of another have been found in the south wall. At each angle there was apparently a circular bastion bonded into the wall and between each bastion and gateway a rectangular turret. The inner and outer faces of the walls were built of squared stones and the space between them filled with layers of flints set in mortar. At intervals bonding courses of tiles were inserted. Large numbers of these stones were used in local buildings after the fort fell out of use.

The outer ditches are crossed by a causeway which would have been the start of Watling Street, the Roman road that was to make its way across country to London, through the Midlands and on to Chester. Their curious appearance south of this gateway is due to a Roman error in cutting them, but this would not have appeared evident on completion in the way that it does today.

On either side of the west gate was a guard chamber, built of large stones taken from the ruins of the monument dismantled from the huge foundation remaining. The north chamber is marked out in concrete but a considerable portion of the south chamber still exists.

The parallel ditches immediately inside the west gate were dug in AD43 and have been traced in both directions for a total of 2,700 feet (820m) but only the short portion visible has been excavated, for they were soon filled in once the progress of the invasion had ensured that it was no longer necessary to defend their base here. The ditches would have been crossed by a bridge in the

Richborough Castle, west wall.

Richborough Castle showing the thickness of the north wall at the north-east corner of site.

alignment of the east-west road through the fort, for the abutments can still be seen. The Romans called this place Rvtvpiae, though why and what was the meaning of the word has never been ascertained.

South of this "bridge" stood the "Chalk House", a fourth century building with walls of blocks of chalk resting on wooden piles. The plan of this building is marked out in concrete, although nothing is known of its purpose. Across the causeway between the triple ditches are two more buildings of note. The brick pillars seen in the ditches to the north are part of the drainage system of the house east of the triple ditches. A house stood on this site in the first century, but most of what can be seen today belongs to a second century rebuilding. The south portion of it consisted of three open courtyards or possibly large covered rooms, used as shops or workrooms, with a veranda in front. At the rear were eight rooms with a corridor. South of the causeway is a fourth century temple with a "cella" to contain the image of the deity and a portico or flight of steps in front. It is interesting to note here how the ground level has risen in some two and a half centuries.

Ahead now is the Great Foundation, the base on which stood a magnificent four-way arch towering 85 feet (25m) high adorned with bronze statues and marble imported from Italy. A model in the museum gives an impression of its original appearance. The concrete cross was the platform for the passageway between the arches, reached by four flights of steps which became victim of subsequent stone robbing. Below the foundation are the outlines of two of ten storehouses or granaries.

Beyond the foundation by the edge of the eastern escarpment is the ground plan of the Saxon Chapel of St Augustine. Medieval legend relates that St Augustine landed here on his way to meet Ethelbert, King of Kent, in 597 and in former days a stone was shown to pious pilgrims which was reputed to retain the imprint of his foot, so the chapel was built to preserve the relic. The chapel consisted of a rectangular chancel and a nave, with an annexe at the west end. The semi-circular apse was added later. The plan is clearly indicated by concrete lines, the varying width distinguishing the different periods. The substantial stone building in the north-east corner of the site was an official building, for the ditches of the third century earth fort stopped short of it. It remained in use until the building of the Saxon Shore Fort when a small military bath building was built on the site. Its remains include a hypocaust, a brick stoke-hole arch and a plunge-bath in the shape of an elongated octagon which are at a higher level. In a late phase the plunge-bath was filled in and covered with tiles, of which about a third has been left in place.

From here it is possible to access outside the north walls where it becomes evident that the wall was built in sections by different construction gangs, and the join between two of the sections is very clear to the east of the north postern. See how the rows of patterning in chalk and ironstone blocks are on different levels in each of the sections.

 At the tower with an opening for a postern gate, its outer face has a large stone which for centuries was called "Queen Bertha's Head" but recent investigation has shown this to be the much worn head and mane of a lion, the rest of which is embedded in the wall. From here it is clear to see a break in the ditches beyond the north wall and it is probable that a bridge crossed here also.

Re-enter the fort through the postern gate, following the length of wall to the north-west corner and passing an hexagonal brick structure on the way. This is a fourth century baptismal font which would have stood inside a timber-built Christian church and is one of the oldest Christian structures in Britain. Further round pass the remains of an early second century wine cellar which would have been entered by a flight of steps and was divided into two rooms. In one were found conical holes in the ground in which amphorae (wine jars) had stood.

Leave the fort through the west gate and turn right as far as the foundations of the first projecting tower. In the corner between the tower and the fort wall can be seen the remains of a tile chute, possibly the discharge from a latrine at a higher level. Walk back past the west gate along the berm, keeping the fort ditches to the right. At the next tower two rows of putlog holes for timber scaffolding are clearly visible, as are four much larger holes at the level of the lower putlog holes. These holes mark the position of timber floor joists, visible here because the front half of the tower has fallen away.

Rounding the south-west corner tower arrive back at the entrance to the site and the small museum. Here the model of the four-way arch and fragments of its marble architectural decoration and bronze statuary occupy the central case. Copies of other important items found on site and now on display in the British Museum are also here.

English Heritage. Opening times: 1st April-30th September, daily 1000-1800. Admission charge.

Route: Follow the approach road and turn left at the metalled road. In about 250 yards (230m) turn left over a stile and cross the railway to a cast-iron gate and another stile. Turn right onto the Saxon Shore Way and the Stour Valley Walk and continue under the viaduct to the road, which follow round left as it joins the A257 to the Gallows Field information board. Gallows Field is where executions took place in former times. Continue ahead along Strand Street into Sandwich. (1.5 miles/2.4km)

SANDWICH. Here is one of the most ancient and historic towns in Kent. Originally built on a sandbank, it was one of the five chosen Cinque Ports in the eleventh century whose chief duty was to provide men and ships for the King's navy. In recognition it received many valuable privileges and was granted two representatives in Parliament; the ports were exempt from taxes; they had their own law courts; and their trade was free of tolls. Most of these privileges were lost in 1688 and the remainder in 1835.

In 1383 the English fleet captured a large French ship carrying a prefabricated wall, 20 feet high, 3,000 feet long with turrets every 12 feet capable of holding ten men each. This was assembled at Sandwich by its inventor, an Englishman, and for a time acted as part of the port defences. In 1451 the Great Bulwark was erected in the south-east corner of the town; this was two storeys high and was well provided with cannon. On the 20th August 1457 Pierre de Breze landed with a French raiding party and captured the Bulwark, but got no further. The Bulwark was never really a castle, but was held by the bastard Fauconberg for the Earl of Warwick during the Wars of the Roses. It was demolished shortly after the Battle of Barnet in 1471.

Edward III used the port frequently and there is mention of a castle here during his reign, but alas no proof today. By the end of the sixteenth century the harbour had silted up, but the town still remained prosperous thanks to an influx of Flemish weavers who left behind a wealth of old buildings.

Guide to the Buildings of Sandwich On the walk into town from Richborough along Strand Street, the first building of note is St Mary's Church which was in danger of being demolished and is now maintained by the Redundant Churches Fund and is usually left open for visitors. The central tower collapsed in 1668, irretrievably damaging the early twelfth century interior. Just beyond the church stands the Old House. This was once a hostel for pilgrims on their way to Canterbury, and is a timber-framed building refaced in brick.

The King's House is where Henry VIII and Elizabeth I are reputed to have stayed. Built in the early fifteenth century it was once by the sea but now stands on the banks of the River Stour. Its interior panelling is worth a fortune.

Along Harnet Street is the Guildhall, a fine timbered building dating from 1579 which has a panelled courtroom, Dutch paintings and the municipal treasures. An oak screen within dates from before Shakespeare and a stained-glass window in the courtroom shows Elizabeth I entering the town. Over the mantelpiece in the Council Chamber is the Charter signed by Charles II making Sandwich a free town for ever.

The Guildhall is only open to visitors by appointment (tel: 01304 617197). Admission charge.

The Guildhall Museum (adjacent) is open 1st April-30th November, Tuesdays, Wednesdays, Fridays and Saturdays 1030-1230 and 1400-1600; Thursdays and Sundays 1400-1600. Admission charge.

Across the old Cattle Market is St Peter's Church which also is no longer in use for worship. The central tower fell in 1661 removing the south aisle, but it does have a preserved seventeenth century tower and a Dutch cupola.

The third of the town's churches, St Clement's, dates from the twelfth century and with its fine Norman tower is now the Parish Church of Sandwich. All three parishes were united in 1940.

Down Fisher Street to the Quay is Fisher Gate, built in 1384 after the French first sacked the town. It is the only remaining town gate and is built of faced flint up to the string course. Above that it was restored by the Coopers Guild in 1560 in Sandwich brick. Further along is the Barbican where a toll was collected from 1759-1977 and was one of a chain of blockhouses set up in the reign of Henry VIII.

Other buildings of note are Manwood Court, the original Grammar School, which was built in 1580 in Sandwich brick with crow-stepped gables. Sandwich brick was made from the local river's mud and can be seen in many of the old buildings all over town. Bartholomew's Hospital Chapel is fairly new, but it does have a stone figure of one of its benefactors, a knight in chain mail with his shield and sword. He is Sir Henry de Sandwich and is 700 years old.

Finally, the Salutation Gardens on the Quay by the Stour is an attractive formal garden planted by Gertrude Jekyll and Edwin Lutyens and completed for Henry Farrer in 1911.

Route: From the Quay proceed down the tree-lined avenue with the Stour on the left. At the end turn left over the footbridge then right. As the Stour bends left, fork right at the Saxon Shore Way marker along the tarmac path. Follow the path towards the sea, along a dyke known as Green Wall to a footbridge over the New Cut. Bear half right and across a minor road before passing through a kissing gate onto the Royal St George's Golf Links, whose famous links course is a venue for several Open Championships. Follow the clearly marked route to the sea. Turn right along the shoreline onto the Saxon Shore Way, past Sandwich Bay Estate. Keep alongside the Royal Cinque Ports Golf Links on the right, past Tenant Hills to the site of Sandown Castle. (4.8 miles/7.8km)

SANDOWN CASTLE.

SANDOWN CASTLE. The Reformation, the Dissolution of the Monasteries and the alliance between France and the Holy Roman Empire made Henry VIII's England liable to attack from across the channel. To counter this threat the south coast was fortified by a series of circular forts designed to hold a captain and twenty- four men. Sandown Castle, at the north end of Deal promenade, was one of the chain built in the sixteenth century and was originally the largest. Colonel Hutchinson, Ireton's cousin, was imprisoned and died here after the Restoration. His wife ably describes the place in her diary: "the walls were four yards thick, yet it rained in through the cracks in them".

The memorial made from the stones of Sandown Castle.

The only time the castle saw any action was in 1648 during the Second Civil War when, along with Deal and Walmer, Sandown Castle was fortified for the king and part of the fleet supplied them with men, munitions and food. The castle held out against attack, but once Deal surrendered Sandown capitulated shortly afterwards.

It has been in ruins since 1863 and in 1894 two flanking gun positions and a central one were blown up by the Royal Engineers because they were unsafe. Its scanty remains can be seen on the beach and are freely accessible at all times. A memorial made from the stones of the castle can be seen at the roadside.

Route: Continue along the promenade, past the Coastguard Station and the pier to Deal Castle. (1.5 miles/2.4km)

DEAL CASTLE. Remaining intact it is a fine example of a Tudor fort. Shaped like a Tudor Rose, it was an arrangement that gave the fort's 145 cannon maximum fire cover and its walls are about twenty feet thick at the base and about ten feet thick at the summit.

A dry moat surrounds six semi-circular bastions and inside there are six smaller bastions, with a top storey from which further guns could be fired. The central stair provided a means of escape as it connects by passages with the outer bastion and there is a sallyport leading into the moat. There was also an oven for heating cannonballs. Above the entrance are machicolations through which

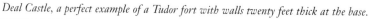

Deal Castle, a perfect example of a Tudor fort with walls twenty feet thick at the base.

grenades could be dropped while attackers were trying to force the portcullis (now gone) and the outer gate.

The only time the castle saw any action was in 1648 during the Second Civil War when Sandown, Deal and Walmer castles were fortified for the king.

During the eighteenth century the present battlements were added for aesthetic reasons and a governor's lodge was constructed on the seaward side. This was rebuilt in 1802 for Lord Carrington but in 1941 a bomb demolished it and the castle was later restored to its original form. An archaeological museum occupies the gatehouse.

English Heritage. Opening times: 1st April-30th September, daily 1000-1800. Admission charge.

Route: Continue along the coastal path past the Lifeboat Station to Walmer Castle. (1 mile/1.6km)

WALMER CASTLE. The original building was constructed in 1539 as a blockhouse and has since been much altered and enlarged. The Lord Warden of the Cinque Ports is also the constable of Dover Castle as the admiral of the ports, and his official residence has been at Walmer Castle since 1708, when it was converted from a fort for this purpose. He still has the right to appoint JPs and the appointment nowadays is a reward for service to the nation. Famous Lord Wardens include the 1st Duke of Wellington, Sir Winston Churchill and Her Majesty Queen Elizabeth the Queen Mother. Admiral Sir Michael Boyce GCB was appointed Lord Warden in 2004.

Oddly, the castle is not that impressive, for its walls, thirteen feet thick, are low, though the moat is deep. It was built by Hugh de Albertsmil and consists of four large bastions with a central circular one. The moat was filled by the sea at high tide.

Enter the castle through its great oak doors, where ominous holes in the roof show where molten lead was dropped to surprise unwelcome visitors. It now has become a museum containing possessions of those who have lived here; Wellington's room is as he left it, and in the middle of the floor is the chair in which he died. Beside it is the camp bed from Waterloo on which he slept when in residence every night, his mattress in its old silk cover and Blucher's velvet blanket over it. The camp chair he used at Waterloo is also here, as are his mirrors and tea cups, boots and some of his letters. There is, too, the reading and writing desk at which he stood to read and write, and the case in which he carried his dispatches in the Peninsular Wars. Also to be seen is his old coffee pot and a picture of Strathfieldsaye, the house in Hampshire given

Walmer Castle, originally built as a blockhouse in 1539 and has been the official residence of the Warden of Cinque Ports since 1708.

to him by the Nation. A copy of *The Times* reports the Battle of Waterloo and there is even a lock of his hair as well as his now famous Wellington boots. With them is Pitt's camp bed and his curious reading chair, some wheelback Hepplewhite chairs in which he sat and an inlaid table on which he played cards and his draftboard.

The magnificent garden, designed by Penelope Hobhouse and given to Her Majesty the Queen Mother on her 95th birthday, is open to public view as are the beautiful gardens surrounding the castle, including the commemorative lawn, woodland walk, croquet lawn, kitchen garden and herbaceous border flanked by mature yew hedges.

English Heritage. Opening times: 1st April-30th September, daily 1000-1800 (1600 on Saturdays); 1st October-31st October, Wednesday-Sunday 1000-1600; 1st March-31st March, daily 1000-1600. Walmer Castle is closed to the public 7th-9th July when the Lord Warden is in residence.

Route: Follow the Saxon Shore Way into Kingsdown, and immediately after the Zetland Arms turn right at the footpath signpost. At the road turn sharp left to continue into Oldstairs Bay, where turn right up the steps and along the cliff top path at Kingsdown Leas. Pass below the Dover Patrol Memorial at Leathercoat Point, which was erected to commemorate the destroyer fleet which, during the First World War, protected the supply routes of the British Army in France. The 90ft high obelisk was unveiled by Edward, Prince of Wales, in 1921. The path continues from behind the Coastguard Station and a footpath goes off left by the viewpoint down into St Margaret's Bay, with its shingle beach which is constantly being carried away by longshore drift, and a succession of groynes which help keep it in place and reduce the risk of promenade erosion. The Coastguard Inn offers toilets and refreshments.

The main route keeps ahead to the road, where a left turn leads down to a sharp bend. Keep ahead here, where the road up from the Bay joins the main route, following the road round left to Pines Garden on the right. (4.2 miles/6.7km)

PINES GARDEN. Nine acres of rare plants in a spectacular setting nestled in a foreland valley which was created on the site of an old rubbish dump by the St Margaret's Bay Trust, and officially opened as a public garden in 1971. With a bog garden and its fine collection of plants, there is also a lake and a statue to Sir Winston Churchill, sculpted by Oscar Nemon on a plinth of Yugoslavian granite. There are also busts of three Roman Emperors, including Julius Caesar, who landed a little way along the coast, and also William I, the last man to successfully lead an invading army into Britain. Other interesting features include a pretty, and old, gypsy caravan, an historic ship's head of Britannica and laid out in turf is the stone façade of the upper section of 73 Cheapside in the City of London, built for the Lord Mayor after the Great Fire of 1666. The windows have been used as small flower beds, making an attractive and unusual design.

Open all year 1000-1700. Admission charge.

Route: Turn right out of the Garden, following the track sharp left and ignoring the track ahead and the path up left as the gardens end on the right. At the top of a short incline keep ahead through the kissing gate before turning right back onto the cliff top path at Lighthouse Down, passing the windmill and two houses. Turn left onto the tarmac road towards South Foreland lighthouse which, although it is no longer used as an aid to navigation, is home to an interesting exhibition and was used for some of Marconi's early broadcasts. Before the white gate, turn left, and at the entrance to the lighthouse continue ahead to a footpath leading towards the sea. At the cliffs turn right and follow the path towards Dover. In about 1 mile (1.6km) keep ahead on the top path after a stile, where an alternative option is to take the short, steep descent into part of Langdon Hole, a dry valley formed by a watercourse that now runs underground in the porous chalk. A steep ascent leads up to the bed of the old railway which was used to transport materials for the building of a prison in 1884 on the site of what is now the car park below the Coastguard Station on top of Fox Hill Down. The prison was converted to an army barracks in 1908 and during World War II, a battery of 16 guns was located on the upper terrace, each of which had an 8 mile (12.8km) range out to sea. Turn left along the old railway towards Dover, and after passing two small caves, fork right onto an ascending narrow track to the car park.

The main route continues to the cross-tracks by the new staircase, where keep straight ahead up the steps. Pass below the Coastguard Station, keeping to the

Saxon Shore Way, before descending to the car park, where the alternative route from Langdon Hole rejoins. Continue above the Outer Harbour, keeping to the Saxon Shore Way as the approach road swings off right, making the steep descent into Dover, passing underneath Jubilee Way to join Marine Parade, bearing right into Townwall Street. Turn right into Woolcomber Street and right again into Castle Hill Road, where the footpath on the right leads to a long staircase at the top of which turn left for the ticket office for Dover Castle. (3.5 miles/5.6km)

DOVER CASTLE. Legend has it that King Harold, whilst residing in Normandy, promised William to build a castle on Dover's eastern cliffs, and this promise he kept, unaware of William's future intentions at the time. During the Battle of Hastings, where Harold was defeated and slain, Dover Castle did not surrender to the Conqueror without much resistance and, according to the legend, its governor Bertram de Ashburnham and his son were cruelly beheaded for their pains. The castle was then given to William's half brother Odo, Bishop of Bayeux, who had played a material part in the victory. He rebelled unsuccessfully against William's successor and so the castle came into the hands of William II and has remained a royal castle ever since.

The first recorded royal visitation was that of Henry II in 1158 and he completely transformed the existing castle, replacing timber defences with stone walls, raised the keep and built the inner ward. The Normans built 27 towers in the outer wall and 14 square watchtowers in the inner wall. The sea cliffs formed the seaward wall so there was no moat, although the entrance bridge straddles a dry ditch. And so Dover Castle became much as we see it today, less the outer curtain wall and its towers - one of the strongest castles in England, which in time earned Kent its proud motto of *"Invicta"*.

Dover Castle on the approach into Dover from South Foreland.

It was Henry II who was instrumental in the murder of Thomas Becket, Archbishop of Canterbury, so it was probably reparation that caused him to build the beautiful little chapel in the castle keep which is dedicated to Thomas Becket and has been refurnished and brought back into use as a place of worship after many centuries of neglect and misuse. It was also Henry II who built the massive keep, 375 feet (114m) above sea level with walls 24 feet (8m) thick at their base and the well 400 feet (121m) deep.

The castle was built on the foundations of an Iron Age fort and within its precincts are the remains of a Saxon fortress and the Roman pharos or light tower, which was once 80 feet (24m) high. Even today its remains are 40 feet (12m) high and are the highest and oldest Roman remains in Britain. The fortress church built by the side of the pharos is that of St Mary-in-Castro and dates back to the tenth and eleventh centuries. So this place has been continuously fortified from the early Iron Age and Roman times until it was de-commissioned in 1958.

Richard Coeur de Lion is believed to have stayed in Dover Castle for the purpose of equipping a fleet en route to the Holy Land and when he died in his last crusade, John was in waiting for his crown. His selfish and extravagant rule began in 1199 and one of the few places remaining loyal during these troubled times was Dover Castle, under the constableship of Sir Hubert de Burgh. The castle was besieged by French forces from June to December 1216 and several times the Dauphin called for the castle to surrender, but each time they refused. Meanwhile the king despatched Sir Stephen de Pencestre to Dover's aid, for he knew the castle well, and while the French were kept busy attacking the western steep, he crept with 400 men-at-arms equipped with heavy crossbows under cover of the eastern hills and approached from a dip of land leading up from the low cliff under the eastern ramparts. They went through a cutting in the embankment to the fosse, where under Sir Adam Fitzwilliam's tower was a sallyport through which they passed to the relief of the gallant Sir Hubert. This was the turning point of the war. The Dauphin was compelled to retreat and bring fresh reinforcements from France, by which time further improvements were made to the castle's defences, including the large earthwork with souterrains and approaches which stretch due north-west from the Norfolk tower. When the Dauphin returned the following spring he was defeated at sea by Sir Hubert before he could even reach land.

During the reign of Henry III the constableship of Dover Castle changed hands many times. After the Battle of Lewes in 1264 in which Henry III was defeated, his son Prince Edward and a host of prisoners were confined in the castle dungeons. When the Prince was liberated the following year, he raised an army and marched on Dover. The prisoners took possession of the "great tower" and rose up against their keepers and assisted Edward in restoring the castle to his father. It was during his reign that the outer curtain wall and towers were added and the church of St Mary was beautified with its Early English arches and decorative detail.

The castle saw happier and more peaceful times when Edward II returned from Spain with his bride Isabella on February 2nd 1308 and the youthful Richard II met his bride, Anne of Bohemia, here in 1382.

In the reign of Henry V the tables were turned and Dover Castle became a firm base for conquest in France. It was to Dover that the victor of Agincourt returned in triumph and it was where Henry VIII stayed with Catherine of Aragon en route to the Field of the Cloth of Gold.

Charles I fitted out the Royal Apartments for the reception of Princess Henrietta Maria of France who arrived in Dover on Sunday 15th June 1625 for her marriage in Canterbury Cathedral. On 23rd February 1642 the same King and Queen, accompanied by their daughter Princess Mary, were again in Dover Castle, but this time in preparation of the Queen sailing to the continent with most of the crown jewels in an attempt to raise money by pawning them in support for her husband's cause.

During the Civil War in August 1642 a Royalist garrison surrendered to a party of 12 Parliamentarians led by a local merchant called Drake. They climbed over the north-east wall and talked the Royalist commander into surrender. Another 120 men marched in from Canterbury and by the time the Royalists had rallied, Drake had the castle secured. The castle was returned to Royalist hands by the Restoration and Charles II kept a magnificent court here, but the last time the castle was used as a royal court was when James II met his bride here on 21st June 1672. With the end of the Stuarts the castle ceased to be used as a royal residence and was handed over to the garrison for military purposes. It was during this period that the beautiful church of St Mary went from neglect to ruin, to be used as a coal store by the mid-eighteenth century.

In 1794 the circular Valence and Mortimer towers were added and another tower, which still remains though in a much altered state, was built over Colton Gate, which leads to the pharos. With the threat of invasion from Napoleon at the turn of the century, the castellated towers of the inner ward were levelled off and filled with rubble to make gun platforms. Lieutenant Burgoyne, Inspector General of Fortifications, installed gun positions on the keep roof, built many bastions and excavated a series of underground passages defended by an ingenious system of remote controlled doors which could trap attackers. Provision was made for a total of 231 guns of all sizes to defend the castle.

Numerous cannon emplacements were built and the castle defences were put in good order for the invasion that never came.

In 1862, with the aid of a government grant and a private bequest, the church of St Mary-in-Castro was finally restored for divine worship.

During the Second World War the castle escaped any serious damage and it was in an extensive series of passageways and rooms carved out of the rock beneath the castle that in 1940 Operation Dynamo, the evacuation of Dunkirk, was masterminded.

Guide to the Castle Enter through:-

1. Canon's Gate which was built in the 1790s at the southern end of the western outer curtain wall. Now proceed north past...

2. Queen Elizabeth's Pocket Pistol is the beautifully embossed 24-foot long cannon which is believed to have been presented to the Queen by the States of Holland. It was made in Utrecht in 1544 by James Tolkyns and is claimed to be capable of throwing a 12lb ball 7 miles (11.2km). The ornamental carriage on which it is mounted dates only from 1827. Now pass through...

3. Peverell's Gate en route to Henry II's inner bailey. Hereabouts the bulk of...

4. Constable's Gate appears on the left, affording the best view of the wall of the inner bailey, with its rectangular mural tower. From the time it was built in the 1220s this gatehouse has been the residence of the constable of the castle or his deputy. The back of the tower, i.e. inside the castle and facing the visitor, was much restored in 1882. Outside, the elegant Georgian sash windows are, of course, alterations, as are the pretty little balcony and the ugly brick casemate between the tall piers of the medieval bridge.

The roadway leading off outside from Constable's Gate affords a splendid view of the castle ditch and bank, the latter being the north-west section of the outer curtain, mostly built by King John, running through Treasurer's, Godsfoe and Crevecoeur Towers and curving round to the three Norfolk Towers, King John's former gateway at the north apex, with St John's Tower standing guard out in front. From this landward side the castle was most vulnerable, at least until all the thirteenth century precautions were taken after the siege of 1216. Beyond all this array of thirteenth century architecture are the twin beaked towers marking the entrance to the...

5. Underground Passages. It was during the Napoleonic Wars between 1793-1815 that miners began burrowing into the chalk cliffs and in all seven tunnels (called casemates) were driven inwards from the cliff face within the castle boundary. The chalk strata, a soft white limestone deposit, the origins of which date back 100 million years, was easy to work and relatively easy to excavate. It was from here in 1940 - in what became known as the Admiralty Casemate nearly 60m below ground level - that Vice Admiral Bertram Ramsay, Flag Officer Dover, secretly masterminded the allied troop evacuation from the beaches of Dunkirk.

Tunnelling began in 1797 to construct underground facilities beneath the castle for accommodation of the garrison, gun crews and stores. Two groups of three parallel tunnels ran in from the cliff face and guns were emplaced at the seaward end of the tunnels while vertical ventilation shafts were cut at the inland end to disperse gun smoke. Access to these tunnels was served by a smaller communication passage linking each of them at the rear. Near the seaward end of the easternmost tunnel a second communication passage was cut behind the cliff face, linking the eastern group to an open area in front of three western tunnels. This was known as "The Terrace" and at its western end a tunnel gradually sloped upwards to ground level to provide an access route for moving heavy guns and equipment into the casemates. By the time these tunnels were finished in 1810 the Napoleonic threat was over and the guns were never mounted.

When war broke out in 1914 the tunnels, having been maintained, were available, but for less exciting storage purposes. World War II brought the underground complex into its own, with enemy occupation only 21 miles (33.7 km) away across the Channel. Vice Admiral Bertram Ramsay and his naval staff moved in to occupy the east casemate in 1939, setting up the first operations room.

By 1941 the movement of enemy shipping was plotted from here and as the war effort expanded, so the tunnels became crammed with communication equipment and its operatives, so it was decided to extend the tunnels slightly above and to the rear of the East Admiralty Casemate. But extensive tunnelling produced several million cubic yards of spoil which had to be disposed of, most of which was dumped in the sea. Unfortunately this showed up clearly on RAF reconnaissance photographs necessitating a long term camouflage policy.

The following year tunnelling recommenced at a lower level beneath the casemates, forming an area of tunnels, passages and rooms which by 1943 became known as "Dumpy". This complex extended outwards from a former Napoleonic magazine reached through an old lift shaft, and was eventually fitted out as a fully equipped operational HQ for the joint services.

After the Second World War everything moveable was cleared from the casemate complex, Annexe and "Dumpy". During the Cold War between the Soviet bloc and the West, the tunnels once again came into prominence, being upgraded to withstand a nuclear attack. "Dumpy" was re-instated to form one of the Regional Seats of Government in the event of a nuclear war and it remained in use until the late 1970s, when the Regional Seat was moved to Crowborough. Once again "Dumpy" was closed and stripped of its equipment and relinquished by the government in 1984. It was taken over by English Heritage who opened the Casemate level to the public in 1990, although the "Dumpy" level is still closed to public view.

6. Fitzwilliam Gate with its twin beaked towers has a caponier or covered passageway across the ditch. Beyond this are the projecting rectangular towers of Henry II's stretch of the outer curtain, terminating in his polygonal Avranches Tower.

7. Inner Bailey This can be entered either through the North Barbican and King's Gate to the north, or through Palace Gate to the south. Along the inside of the bailey walls once stood a complex of medieval domestic apartments. The present buildings of 1745 incorporate some of their walls, preserve much of their plan and on the east show a little detail of Henry III's time.

8. Keep The dominating feature of the inner bailey is the keep which rises to a height of 95 feet and measures 98 feet by 96 feet in area. Its walls of Kentish ragstone dressed with stone from Caen in Normandy are of immense thickness, varying from 21 feet at the base to 17 feet. The building is given even greater solidity by an internal cross-wall which divides it into roughly two equal halves within and helps carry the weight of the roof. Above a basement, used mainly for storage and cooking, are two residential floors, each level connected by two wide stairways, one in the north-east angle and one in the south-west, extending from basement to roof. Each floor was a self-contained suite of apartments on a grand medieval scale, comprising of two very large rooms, serving as the Great Hall and Great Chamber, with lesser chambers opening off them. The second residential floor was much the grander and was doubtless intended for the King's use or visitors of an important rank.

The principal entrance to the keep is also at this second floor level, reached through the forebuilding, which is one of the most impressive in all England. It consists of three flights of steps ascending round two sides of the keep through three turrets or lesser towers which project from the main block of the building. Each flight of steps was originally open to the sky so that it could be defended by covering fire from the top of the tower above it. Near the foot of the first flight of steps is an entrance straight into the basement. At the top of this first flight of steps is the lower vestibule of the forebuilding, elegantly arcaded on the southern side, with a porter's lodge on the right behind a beautiful lower chapel.

From the lower vestibule turn sharp left to ascend two further flights of steps, with a drawbridge pit between them, now crossed by modern steps and a bridge, at the approach to the second and central turret of the forebuilding.

At the foot of the first stairway, on the left, is a fifteenth century doorway leading into the first floor apartments, now the custodian's office. At the top of the second there is an upper entrance vestibule, with a guardroom ahead and on the left the great doorway into the second floor apartments, carved and moulded as befits the entrance to state apartments. Through this doorway, on the left of the entrance passage, is the well chamber, and to the left of the well head is a recessed stone sink in which can still be seen the mouths of two leaden pipes intended to convey water to other parts of the keep. While the well itself is an impressive engineering achievement, the refinement of a piped water supply in a twelfth century building is nothing short of remarkable.

At the end of the entrance passage steps lead down into the second floor apartments. Here are two very large rooms, inter-connected by a doorway at the northern end of the cross-wall and a passageway and chamber at the southern end. The walls of both rooms are marked with *graffiti* by French prisoners of war. The first room has a curious feature of an archway 5 feet above the floor and set in modern brick, opening into a small mural chamber whose use is unknown. The other room has a fifteenth century fireplace

The Dover Patrol Memorial at Leathercoat Point, 90ft high unveiled by the Prince of Wales in 1921.

unaltered, though restored, with Edward IV's Yorkist badges of the rose *en soleil*. On the right of its west window a doorway leads into the King's bedchamber.

The chapel of this second floor is reached through the mural chambers and passages leading off from the southern window embrasures of the two great rooms. At the end of a narrow passage is the sacristy on the right, while on the left is first an ante-chapel and then the chapel proper. All are richly decorated with wall arcades, arches with chevron ornament, carved capitals and groined vaults.

The first floor can be reached by either of the two great spiral stairways. Its residential accommodation is laid out almost exactly the same as that on the second floor, though its chapel can only be reached by passing through what is now the custodian's office and crossing the lower vestibule of the forebuilding. Each of the two large main apartments has its fifteenth century fireplace more or less intact, with the Yorkist badges, which are dead centre of the cross-wall. The eastern apartment contains a fine scale model of the battlefield of Waterloo, which was made in the 1830s by Captain William Siborne.

The basement is naturally gloomy, with a basic plan of two main central rooms with mural chambers opening off. The main rooms are smaller than those upstairs because of the thickness of the walls, but more room has been achieved by piercing the cross-wall with three large archways. A long and narrow mural chamber, containing a great oven, is reached by a passage from the north-east stairway.

A spiral stairway leads up to the roof, where there are traces of mountings of the heavy guns of the post-medieval period and terrific panoramic views of the castle, Dover, the harbour, the surrounding countryside and, on a clear day, the coast of France.

Leaving the inner bailey ahead is the church of St Mary-in-Castro beside which is…

9. The Pharos The top 19 feet (6m) are medieval, the result of alterations by Humphrey, Duke of Gloucester, between 1415-1437, but the lower 43 feet (13m) are good Roman work. Built of flint rubble it was originally faced in ashlar blocks with external brick bonding-courses. The outer face, octagonal in plan, is now much battered by decay and medieval refacing. In Roman times it rose in a series of eight vertical stages with an offset of 1 foot (30cm) at each stage. It was probably about 80 feet (25m) high when built, which is 20 feet (6m) higher than it is today, and from its top a beacon of fire would have burned by day and night to guide ships using the Channel.

The Roman entrance still survives on the south side, and some of the upper windows retain their stone voussoirs interlaced with brick. The square interior is now a roosting place for pigeons. It was probably built in the second century, although it could date from as early as the first century. Each storey had a wooden floor, the first being 17.5 feet (5.35m) above ground level and the others at intervals of about 8 feet (2.4m). Its partner on the opposite Western Heights has now disappeared.

English Heritage. Opening times: 1st April-30th September, daily 1000-1800 (open 0930 in August); 1st -31st October, daily 1000-1700; 1st November-31st January, Thursday-Monday 1000-1600; 1st February-31st March, daily 1000-1600. Closed 24th -26th December & 1st January. Admission charge.

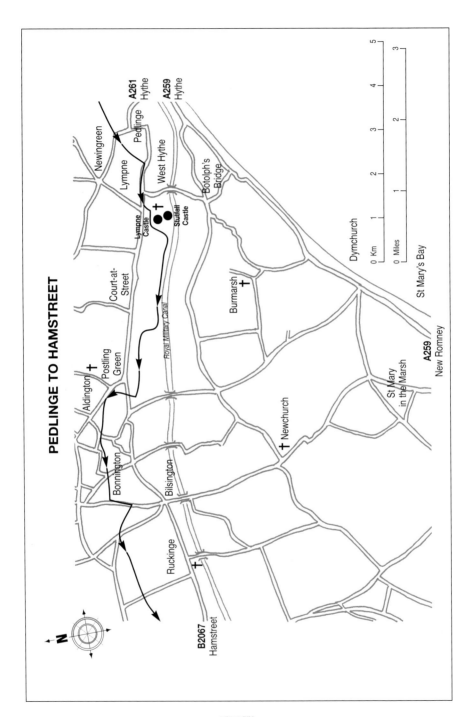

PEDLINGE TO HAMSTREET

Newingreen
A261 Hythe
Pedlinge
A259 Hythe
Lympne
West Hythe
Botolph's Bridge
Lympne Castle
Stutfall Castle
Court-at-Street
Royal Military Canal
Burmarsh
Postling Green
Aldington
Bonnington
Newchurch
Bilsington
St Mary in the Marsh
A259 New Romney
Ruckinge
B2067 Hamstreet
Dymchurch
St Mary's Bay

0 Km   1   2   3   4   5
0 Miles   1   2   3

N

30

Dover to Lympne Castle

This section continues to follow the coastline west of Dover along Shakespeare Cliff and looking down on Samphire Hoe, made from the spoil of creating the Channel Tunnel. At Capel-le-Ferne the route leaves the coast to circumnavigate Folkestone, making its way to Castle Hill before skirting the new Eurotunnel Terminal and dropping down on unspoilt Newington. Saltwood castle stands in natural camouflage behind Hythe and then it's on to Lympne, whose castle occupies a commanding position overlooking the Royal Military Canal.

ROMAN PAINTED HOUSE. Clearly signposted and reached via Castle Hill Road, keeping ahead at the traffic lights into Castle Street then right at Market Square into Cannon Street then left into New Street.

Here was the discovery of another fort, built for a garrison of 700 men on a slightly different site in the second century, which was totally unexpected. Evidence of numerous tiles stamped CL BR makes it certain that this was one of the Headquarters of the British fleet, the *Classis Britannica*. Excavations have shown that the first fort of 117-120AD was never finished but replaced by a new fort of AD130, with re-buildings going on until around 210.

In 1971 part of a building was discovered in the extensive civilian settlement which grew up in the second and third centuries north of the *Classis Britannica* fort. Parts of five rooms, all with hypocausts, together with a corridor, were salvaged. They were built around 200AD over an earlier building of around 150AD of which part of one room is also visible. The walls, still standing 10 feet/3m high in places, are covered with brightly coloured painted plaster, exceptionally well preserved in one room and part of a second. Substantial finds of painted wall plaster in situ in Britain are extremely rare, indeed Dover can boast the only large area of Roman wall plaster (over 400 square feet/37.2 square metres) still in place on the walls where it was painted 1800 years ago. It was first opened to the public in 1977.

Guide to the Remains: On entering look down on the Saxon Shore fort defences, well preserved to the left, but scant on the right. Beyond are the remains of the "Painted House", its amazing state of preservation due to the burial of the rooms under an earth bank behind the wall of the Roman fort, the construction of which removed most of the rest of the earlier building. Room 3 is in the foreground and room 2 beyond; the latter is extremely well preserved apart from a breach in the far wall. But it is the frescoed walls which catch the eye in both these rooms.

Above a dado of red or green is a series of white panels framed predominantly in yellow and red and flanked by elegant columns in perspective, of which the lower parts and bases are visible. The objects on the perspective "shelf" in front of these panels include a torch, a vine tendril, a basket and a Bacchic wand (thyrsus) repeated several times round the walls of rooms 2, 3 and 4. Fallen fragments from room 3, displayed in a case on the upper level, show that here the white panels were occupied by human figures; probably Bacchus and his female companions, the Maenads.

The number of hypocausts in this building would suggest it was part of a public building or *mansio*, an official inn for travellers of high rank.

Moving left past the diorama of Roman Dover with its forts and twin lighthouses, go downstairs to a display case of unusual finds, where facing you are the remains of room 1, with a channelled hypocaust built of limestone blocks capped with flint tiles. There are no surviving frescoes in this room, but moving round are three impressively preserved brick flue-arches, of which only the left one shows evidence of substantial use. The walling here stands 10 feet (3m) high, and even part of the external rendering, painted red, is still intact. The lower walls in front of you clearly belong to an earlier structure and one is actually incorporated into the walling of the Painted House. The room to the left seems to have been a later addition, because it masks the flue at this point.

Pause at the corner to observe the fresco in room 4 and the foundation trench of the Saxon Shore fort which sliced through it and now walk round to the other side of the projecting tower, noting how it rests on the demolished remains of room 5 of the Painted House. The room had a channelled hypocaust of the same type as in room 1. Massive building blocks were thrown on the floor of this room to provide an adequate foundation for the third century defences, and here you can see the well-preserved facing of the Roman fort wall, nine courses high and over 8 feet (2.5m) thick. The tower is not bonded with the curtain wall so was obviously a later addition, though how much later is uncertain.

Just outside the façade of the building adjacent to the Roman Painted House are the remains of the north part of the east gate of the *Classis Britannica* fort of 130AD, and a projecting tower added to the Saxon Shore fort of 270AD adjacent to it at a higher level. This spot marks one of the points where the defences of the two forts intersected. The semicircular front of the *Classis Britannica* gate-tower, projecting forward from the line of the walls, is a feature highly unusual at this date, and the Dover fort was obviously a prestige monument, designed to impress, for the whole gate was originally 41 feet (12.5m) wide. These Roman structures can easily be viewed by looking over the low wall on York Street at the south-west corner of the modern building.

In 1970 further excavations revealed nine barracks, two granaries and a latrine and in 1990 part of another building within the fort were discovered. Further excavations are still ongoing.

Opening times: April-September, daily (except Monday) 1000-1700. Admission charge. Tel: 01304 203279

Route: Turn left into York Street, crossing over at the traffic lights and turning left then right into Snargate Street past The Grand Shaft.

THE GRAND SHAFT

was built as a short cut between Dover and the Western Heights for troops stationed in the barracks above, and is a unique 140-foot triple spiral stairway dug through the cliffs between 1806-9. The Western Heights consisted of areas of moats, ditches, bastions, batteries and forts, built mainly during the Napoleonic Wars.

Opening times: not confirmed. Admission charge.

Route: Follow the footpath to the next roundabout, following the signs for Cycle Route 2 and turning off left at the underpass by the North Downs Way signpost. Turn right and follow the enclosed path along the cliff edge: eventually the path joins the tarmac cycle route, which follow almost to the road. Turn left at the North Downs Way signpost about 20 yards (18m) before the road, along an enclosed path to the cliff top. Pass the Cliff Top Café at Capel-le-Ferne, returning to the path from the car park. Turn left at the concrete track and right in 20 yards (18m) at the North Downs Way sign, down the steps and then up again. Pass the Battle of Britain Memorial to continue along the cliff top path to where the path turns sharp right away from the cliff edge to emerge at the road by the Valiant Sailor public house. Cross the road with care to continue through a kissing gate by the North Downs Way sign, passing to the right of a trig point with Folkestone visible on the left. Just before the communication mast it becomes necessary to join the road and at the crossroads cross the stile on the left to continue along the North Downs Way, past the mast on the right. The route then hugs the fence alongside the road until a stile leads onto the road, which follow downhill to the road. Cross straight over to continue through the kissing gate to the left of Crete Road West. Where the path splits, take the left fork, climbing up with Sugarloaf Hill on the left and Castle Hill ahead. (8 miles/12.8km)

CASTLE HILL (FOLKESTONE).

Much of Folkestone Downs is now owned by Eurotunnel. The massive earthworks on Castle Hill are the remains of

The Eurotunnel rail terminal as viewed from the summit of Castle Hill.

a Norman ringwork and bailey castle, probably built in the early 1140s. It is one of the largest and most complete ringwork and bailey castles in south-east England. There is no evidence to prove there were any settlements on Castle Hill before the Normans, and although known locally as "Caesar's Camp" the earthworks are known to have been built a thousand years after the Romans.

A ringwork of earth banks and ditches would have provided the main defence to a wooden bailey. Within the ringwork the main residential buildings and a chapel would have been built. A raised causeway joins the ringwork and bailey, leaving the site for 100m. This would have been the only entrance to the castle. The bailey would have housed soldiers and contained store areas, stables and workshops.

Castle Hill (Folkestone) with its two ditches clearly visible around its summit. It was probably built in the early 1140s.

Below the Norman earthworks is another, more recent, defensive ditch. This "tank trap" was dug at the start of World War II in 1940.

The only excavation of Castle Hill took place in 1878 and was conducted by General Pitt Rivers. Pottery and flints from the late Neolithic (Stone Age) period, about 4,000 years ago, were found, and Roman coins were discovered nearby. There are scars on the south side of the site which are the only remains today of Pitt Rivers' dig.

Route: The path passes to the left of Castle Hill, overlooking the Eurotunnel Rail Terminal. Drop down under the power lines to the road, to continue left along the North Downs Way path and as it opens out into a field, take the right fork up to a metal gate. The path soon runs alongside the road, passing the junction off right to Hawkinge. The path now crosses to a road where turn left downhill, leaving the North Downs Way (although we shall be re-joining it again much later in the walk). Turn off left at the public footpath signpost, crossing the field to the left, then turn right onto an old trackway, forking left into Newington. (2.75 miles/4.5km)

NEWINGTON. Formerly known as Newington-juxte-Hithe is where the Georgian cottages opposite the church gates were once the village workhouse and opposite the village shop can be seen the village pound. The twelfth century Norman church dedicated to St Nicholas houses three great possessions: a pair of small windows, a magnificent pulpit and a group of brasses arrayed on the nave walls. The brasses have around twenty portraits on them, including an unusual one to Christopher Reittenger, who was physician to the Tsar of Russia and died in 1612. The pulpit is a fascinating legacy of the fifteenth century, though the eight carved panels seem to have been made from a screen. The old almsbox with its three locks comes from the same period.

Route: Take the road left in front of the church, past Church House, to continue along the footpath ahead. Turn right at the stile and left at the road, under the bridges before crossing the road to continue right at the public bridleway signpost. Cross the M20 then right along a metalled track, turning left in 100 yards (91m), under the railway to continue along a delightful metalled bridleway. Turn right beyond the training base, through the gate and across the next field diagonally right to the woods. Continue through the wood to Sene Barn, where turn right to the road. Left at the road, past Sene Valley Golf Course and into the boundary of Hythe. Ignore the footpath off right, but a little further down the hill turn off right at the public bridleway (opposite Bassett Close) where the towers of Saltwood Castle can be seen in the trees. Follow the path into the Estate, following the track round left then right to the farm building. Turn left under the bridge then right, past Saltwood Castle. (2 miles/3.2km)

SALTWOOD CASTLE. It is recorded that Aesc, son of Hengist, built a castle in this place in 488, but during the Roman occupation it was considered so important they made it a fortified port, as Hythe at that time was still under water. The present castle was built by Henry de Essex, Henry II's standard bearer but, accused of cowardice in battle, Essex became a monk and the castle reverted to the Crown. It was already the joint property of Becket, Archbishop of Canterbury, and the Warden of the Cinque Ports, formerly Henry de Essex himself, and when a quarrel broke out between Becket and Henry II about the castle it resulted in a tragic episode in English history. The king's nominee at Saltwood was Randolph de Broc who was also an enemy of the Archbishop and at the king's request he sheltered Robert Fitzurse, Hugh de Moreville, William de Tracy and Richard le Bret, the four knights who landed from Normandy on the 28th December 1170 and murdered Becket at Canterbury the following day. Afterwards they returned to Saltwood and the following morning rode the 40 miles to South Malling, near Lewes, then on to Knaresborough, a fortress in the possession of Hugh de Moreville, where they remained for a year. Fitzurse passed over to Ireland, but his name lingered long in his native Somerset; Moreville died in his bed, leaving two daughters to succeed him. The sword he wore during the murder was kept at Brayton Castle twixt Whitehaven and Carlisle but was twisted and charred by a fire which burned the castle down about a century ago. Bret's end was peaceful and from his family came, as a penitential offering, the Priory of Woodspring, whose ruins can still be seen on the Bristol Channel at a promontory known as St Thomas's Head, surrounded by land given by Bret's granddaughter "in the hope that the intercession of the glorious martyr might never be wanting to her or her children."

Tracy became Justiciary of Normandy and is reputed to have made a pilgrimage to the Holy Land and finally retired to end his days in seclusion

Saltwood Castle. Secluded and privately owned.

near Exeter, where a farmhouse called Woollacombe Tracy is believed to mark the scene of his banishment and death.

Saltwood Castle returned to the Archbishop of Canterbury to become their principal palace and so it remained until the Reformation. Today it is privately owned and very rarely opened to the public, although its imposing

Battle of Britain memorial at Capel-le-Ferne.

twin towers of the outer curtain wall are easily visible and the walk follows the wall round to the magnificent fourteenth century gatehouse.

Route: Following the path to the right of the castle, turn right at the road and after a few paces turn left into the farmyard of Grange Farm. Follow the farm road uphill between the barns to a gate beside the barn ahead. Cross the field to the church.

CHURCH OF ST PETER & ST PAUL.
Dating from the twelfth century, the church has an embattled and turreted tower, Norman windows and doorways and an arch carved with large and small chevrons. Inside its possessions include an oak chest almost eight feet long, three brasses, stone heads on either side of the altar and a fifteenth century font.

Route: Follow the path through the churchyard to the road, where turn left. Right at the Green into Sandling Road then left at the public footpath signpost (Darkies Lane), turning off right into the playing fields and heading diagonally left to the lane. Left at the lane, through the kissing gate and follow the path round right, over the stream and up the next field to the trees on the skyline. Go up a flight of steps and across the next field, heading to the right of the copse ahead. Keep along the edge of the field and over the stile by the old chapel, following the track down to the A261 which cross by Pedlinge Farm. Continue down the track opposite, and just after the farm pond, cross a stile into the field ahead. Head diagonally left across the field to a gate and onto a track where turn right. Where the track bears sharp left at a waymarker, follow the path ahead across fields to the road. Turn right here, following the road for almost half a mile (800m) past the Shepway Cross. (2.5 miles/4km)

SHEPWAY CROSS.
Where the road rises it meets a lane climbing the hillside from the sea. An elegant, slender cross here bears a delicate carving of the Crucifixion. It was presented in 1923 by the Warden of the Cinque Ports to mark the site of the medieval Shepway Cross. The Shepway, a corruption of

Shepway Cross, presented by the Warden of the Cinque Ports in 1923, marks an ancient route from Portus Lemanis to Canterbury.

The old chapel at Pedlinge where the route crosses the A261.

The route over Crete Down and the A20 with Sugarloaf Hill on the right.

"sheepway", was an ancient route on the line of the Roman road from Portus Lemanis to Canterbury. It gave its name to the ancient Court of Shepway, which had jurisdiction over the whole of Romney Marsh. In 1358 the court was attended by 65 barons of the Cinque Ports; today it is presided over only by the Lord Warden of the Cinque Ports.

Route: When the road levels out, turn left down the drive signposted Lympne Church and Castle. (0.5 mile/0.8km)

LYMPNE CASTLE. The castle stands beside the low, massively-walled Norman church of St Stephen, and in the corner of the churchyard are the graves of two pilots who were killed in the Battle of Britain. Lympne Airfield, now Ashford Airport, was home to fighters in both World Wars.

The castle's clifftop vantage position commands views over the marsh and across the Channel to the French coast. It incorporates the Square Tower, which is very old and is believed to be the Roman watch-tower for its Saxon shore fort 300 feet below. From the eleventh century Lympne was granted to the archdeacons of Canterbury. The Great Hall, built in 1360, replaced an early Norman construction of the late eleventh century and the Great Tower was built between 1360 and 1420. Minor restoration work was undertaken in 1905 by Sir Robert Lorrimer, who also built the New Wing, but most of the castle lies untouched since the fourteenth century. Arguably, Lympne is not a castle at all but a fortified residence built for the Archdeacon of Canterbury, for it has no moat or curtain wall, but its towers and its position on the cliff edge would have provided some security from French raiders, and that was probably the reason for the west

Lympne Castle as seen from the main gate.

tower's construction in 1380. Today the castle is privately owned and only open to the public for private functions.

The Norman church of St. Stephen beside the outbuildings of Lympne Castle.

HAMSTREET TO BIDDENDEN

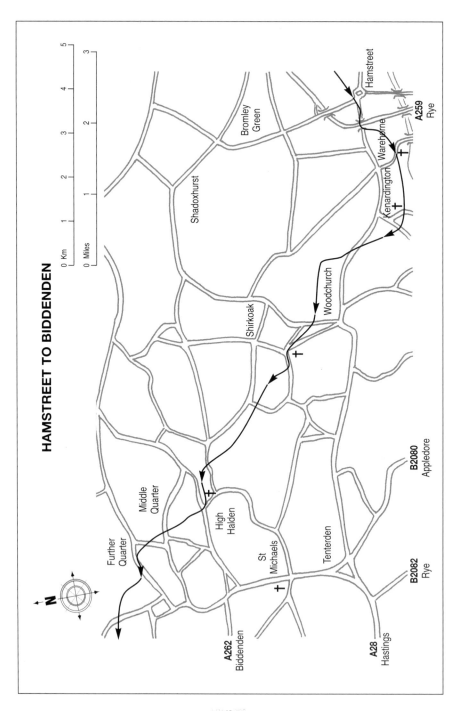

Lympne Castle to Sissinghurst Castle

This is the longest section between castles, although passing the haphazard remains of the ancient Roman fort of *Lemanis*, hanging on the slope beneath Lympne, before following a length of the Royal Military Canal. Back on the Saxon Shore Way it skirts Aldington church then passes through Park Wood, Priory Wood and Dicker's Wood before joining the Greeensand Way on the outskirts of Ham Street Wood. Once through the neighbouring villages of Warehorne and Kenardington we finally leave the Saxon Shore Way, heading further inland to Woodchurch, High Halden and the visually perfect Biddenden. From here it is but a stone's throw to the lovely setting of Sissinghurst.

Route: Continue along a road past the castle gatehouse and when it makes a sharp right turn, turn left down a footpath for 300 yards (275m) to a path running downhill on the left, past the site of Stutfall Castle.

The entrance range of Sissinghurst Castle still used by the Nicholson family.

STUTFALL CASTLE. It once enclosed 10 acres of fortress, built to protect the natural harbour the Romans called *Portus Lemanis*, but its walls today have been much tossed around by landslides and the sea that once lapped its perimeter has now retreated far away. And yet the overgrown ruins that still remain bear an air of impressive solitude. Some fragments are still 25 feet (7.5m) high and 14 feet (4.25m) thick, even though they have fallen from their original positions. The walls originally formed an irregular pentagon and tile-courses and projecting towers (a good example of which still survives on the north-west of the site) make it contemporary with Richborough (perhaps late 270s) although pottery found here indicated there was a naval base here early in the second century. The garrison in the final period is recorded as the *numeri Turnacensium*, recruited in the Tournai region of Belgium, but no interior buildings of this period are visible today. The fort was evacuated and abandoned around 340/350 as the sea receded, the river changed its course and the harbour merely became part of the marsh. Excavations in 1976-8 revealed some further details of the fort, but these have since been backfilled. Part of the east gate has been left exposed, including the large flagstones of the entrance passage and the more southerly of the two solid semi-circular towers which flanked it (now about 2 feet/0.6m high and lying at an angle of 45 degrees thanks to subsidence and landslips) but none of this is now accessible.

Route: Cross the plank bridge before continuing on to the embankment of the Royal Military Canal. (0.75 mile/1.2km)

ROYAL MILITARY CANAL. It was begun in 1804 to protect the coast against the then very real threat of a Napoleonic invasion. Nelson's victory at Trafalgar established the supremacy of the English fleet, which took control of the Channel. The invasion was prevented and the canal was never put to the test. Today it is a tranquil waterway useful for draining the marsh and a habitat for dragonflies and waterbirds.

Route: Turn right alongside the Royal Military Canal. Where the way ahead becomes a gravel road, turn sharp right over a stile back on the Saxon Shore Way. Follow the feint path with waymarkers confirming the route, past the ruins of an old chapel where bear left to a track. Left here, following the Saxon Shore Way to a gate below a new house. Turn left here along a green track, through a gate and alongside trees on the right and then on the left to a marker post at the bottom of the field. Turn right, over a stile and alongside a hedge on the left. Over another stile then turn right along the edge of the field and in 100 yards (91m) right again into trees. Turn right out of the trees and along the edge of a field to a road, where turn right and in 70 yards (65m) left at the footpath signpost. Through the gap to continue straight across the field to the road where turn left with Aldington church to the right. The church has one of the finest sixteenth century Perpendicular towers in the county and remains of its old Saxon tower can still be seen in the vestry. Inside, the chancel is seen through its great arch with a reading-desk on either side and the pulpit with its remarkable carved pelican. The choir stalls have ten lovely bays on each side, the massive poppyheads superbly carved, and six of the stalls have fine misereres. Most of the woodwork has come from the great houses that have vanished hereabouts. The iron gate and screen leading into the tower is modern, but the brass of a man, a woman and three children is fifteenth century. One of the bells in the belfry dates back to 1774. Aldington church is just down Church Lane but is only open on Wednesday mornings and Sundays.

Turn off left at the footpath signpost just past Church Lane, through the gate in the far right corner to continue diagonally right across the next field to a stile beyond the pylon. Turn left along the edge of the next field to a stile but do not cross the stile into the Nature Reserve, instead turn right alongside it to another stile by a row of trees. Follow an obvious path to a stile to the left of a bungalow, then out to the road. Left at road and right at signpost to Mill Road. Turn left at the Saxon Shore Way signpost just past Cloud End, over the stile and sharp right across the field to another stile and on to a third leading onto a lane. Left at the lane and off to the left round Hungry Hall to continue ahead before turning off right over a stile at the start of a short enclosed path. Follow the path to Cherry Orchard Lane where turn right then left signposted Bilsington, turning off right at the footpath signpost in 50 yards (45m) towards the wood.

Go through the wood, taking left fork at waymarker. Bear right out of wood, keeping alongside wood on right and at lane turn left. Immediately beyond Keepers Cottage turn right at signpost into woods. Follow waymarkers through wood, turning left at T-junction and out to road. Straight across road to continue diagonally left then right into more woods. Cross an open field before re-entering the wood, turning right onto a track.

Immediately after a stile by a metal gate turn left over a stile hidden in the bushes then proceed straight across the field to the right of the house on the skyline. Turn left at road past the house then right at the footpath signpost, over a stile and alongside the hedge on the right. Along an enclosed path, bearing left onto the concrete approach road to Gill Farm. Left at the gravel track and right at the English Nature board for Ham Street Woods. Bear right at the wooden gate, keeping to the main track and following Saxon Shore Way markers. The Way then becomes a gravel path then a metalled lane into Hamstreet.

Turn right into Dukes Meadow and straight over at the crossroads by Duke's Head Inn. Under the railway and A2070 before turning up left at the Saxon Shore Way signpost, up the steps and along an enclosed path. Turn right over the stile and alongside the fence on the right, taking a straight route into Warehorne. (10.25 miles/16.5km)

WAREHORNE. The church of St Matthew was built in the thirteenth century and contains pillars of the local Bethersden marble, but its real

treasures are in its windows which are well over 600 years old. Opposite is the sixteenth century Woolpack Inn where, in the mid-1930s the last of the ancient Courts Baron were held. At these courts all who owed "Suit and Service" to the lord of the manor attended to pay their dues, a practice which had succeeded for centuries. As the Court Baron passed out of existence the lady of the manor marked its passing with the gift of the village green to the people for ever.

Route: Keep ahead out of the village, turning off left as the road swings off right and turning right through a gate in a few steps. Straight ahead across two fields, then diagonally left towards the church in the trees. After passing a belt of small trees, head left of another line of trees to cross three bridges over the dykes before continuing ahead to the church of St Mary, Kenardington. (1 mile/1.6km)

KENARDINGTON.

KENARDINGTON. Also known as Kenarton, the name is derived from the Anglo-Saxon name of Kenward or Kinard. The *ing* refers to the family and *ton* quite simply means homestead, thereby Kenardington means "the homestead of the Kinard family". The practice of adding *ing* and *ton* started in the late seventh century and the church stands on the site of a small Saxon fort which was probably built to oppose the Danes but was incomplete when they sacked the site in 892AD.

The church would originally have been built of wood and replaced by stone after the Norman Conquest, for there are remnants of early Norman stonework in the eastern wall of the chancel and the tower dates from 1170. The unusual narrow round tower on the north side carries the staircase to the belfry at the top of the main tower. Legend has it the church was burned by the French in the fourteenth century, but there is no remaining evidence of this, although it is known to have been struck by lightning in 1559, causing the nave, chancel and north aisle to collapse. The remains of the ruined building were used to rebuild the north wall of the south aisle, thus creating the present church. There is a list of Rectors dating back to 1283.

Route: Here we leave the Saxon Shore Way, following the flagstone path right behind the church, over the stile and alongside a fence on the left. Another couple of stiles lead down to the road where turn right and then left at the public footpath signpost opposite the cottages. Head diagonally right across both fields and to the left of the houses, emerging at the road by the goalposts. Cross straight over to continue along a track serving several houses, keeping ahead across three fields (and alongside one). At the wood turn right along the edge of the field just crossed, passing through into the next field at the gap in the left corner to continue diagonally right to a stile near the far left hand corner. Cross the stile and bear left across the next field to a stile leading onto the road. Cross straight over into wood, following path to a clearing where turn left to continue alongside the wood on the left and then on the right. Follow a well-defined path to the road, where turn right into

WOODCHURCH. The village is built around the triangular green and the thirteenth century church of All Saints has an unusually tall shingled spire. Inside is a small brass by the pulpit to the priest Nicholas de Gore, dated 1320, which is the third oldest in Kent, with only sixteen older in all England. The recently rebuilt smock mill stands to the north of the village and the Bonny Cravat Inn, by the gates to the church, is one of the village's more notable buildings.

Route: Turn left out of the churchyard and left again at Susan's Hill. Immediately after the new house turn right over the ladder stile at the green metal gates then over a second stile to continue diagonally left across the field to another stile in the far left corner. Through the copse and along the right edge of the field, then over a stile and along the left edge of the next. Follow the edge of the field round right to a kissing gate off left, then over a succession of fields and stiles to a lane where turn left then almost immediately right through a gate. Over three stiles in quick succession then across a long field and into a copse. Keep to the left of the trees and maintain a straight direction through the organic farm. Down the steps and over a stile to continue straight across the next field with a wood on the left. Cross straight over at road, following a series of stiles and keeping to the right edge of fields to the church at High Halden. (3 miles/4.8km)

HIGH HALDEN. Overlooking the Beult Valley, it has the thirteenth century church of St Mary with its extraordinary timbered porch, a relic of the days when the village was surrounded by a great forest and had timber to spare. Its walls are made of upright timbers 10 feet high, supporting a red tiled roof, from which rises a shingled tower and spire, all made from 50 tons of local oak. In the south porch are more remarkable timbers, two halves of an upturned tree forming an arch. Round the columns in the church are quaint old seats made from Kent marble and there are traces of Norman work in the walls of the nave. The font dates back to the twelfth century.

Up on the A28 the Chequers Inn dates back to 1620 and was where the Ransley gang, a band of notorious smugglers, met in the mid-eighteenth century.

Route: Right out of the churchyard to the A28. Cross over to the Chequers Inn and turn left, turning right immediately before Hathewolden Grange at the public footpath signpost, taking the right fork at the open field and cross stile. Keep diagonally left across next field, through gap in hedge and head for stile in bottom left corner of next field. Diagonally left across third field then cross two stiles to road where turn left and in 75 yards (68m) right immediately after the white building, skirting the wood on the left to another road. Right here then left at the public footpath signpost opposite Beulah, keeping left of the farm pond to the road by Further Quarter. Follow the road left until turning off right at the bridleway signpost as the road bends left, following it round right then left along a green lane past Wagstaff to the road. Cross straight over and follow the footpath alongside the fence on the left to the next road where turn left then right at the T-junction (signposted Biddenden). Just beyond Thousand Acre Farm turn right at public footpath signpost, over stile and diagonally left across field. Over a series of waymarked stiles into Biddenden, turning left at the road and right at the green to the church. (5.5 miles/8.8km)

BIDDENDEN. This is an old Wealden village flanked by fifteenth to seventeenth century half-timbered houses once used for the weaving of cloth. It is famous in legend for the Siamese twin sisters Eliza and Mary Chalkhurst who were born here in 1100 joined at their shoulders and hips and lived for 34 years. They left 20 acres of land to the village of which the income has for centuries been spent on the distribution of bread and cheese to the poor at Easter, and this practice still takes place in the Old Workhouse, local pensioners now being the recipients. The story of the Biddenden Maids is depicted on the village sign and centred round its green, a small patch planted with shrubs, its monuments are admirably grouped. Facing each other stand Hendon House and Hendon Hall both ancient places. The Hall is now a farm while the House has a fine old garden and a sun dial of 1623. The wrecked windmill, the church tower, the black and white houses, the tithe barn and the vicar's pond complete a splendid village group, while on one of the Tudor houses near the church is a painted figurehead from a ship of the Spanish armada. A little way from the square is the old Cloth Hall, a remarkable house of seven gables; Standen Farmhouse was once a monastery; Wackenden was a moated manor at the time of the Norman Conquest; Birchley is a seventeenth century house in a park and Castweasle is a seventeenth century farm.

The Church tower is from around 1400, but the chancel arch and the arches of the nave are at least a century older. The magnificent roof and some of the windows are over 500 years old; the pulpit is 300 years old. There is a fifteenth century oak door to the vestry and there are some good carved faces but the oak screen is fairly modern. The portrait gallery is a prize possession, with brasses of about seventy husbands, wives and children.

Route: Take the footpath behind the church to the T-junction, where turn right, following the path left and forking left where the path passes a new housing development, turning right as the path joins from the left. Keep ahead along the road, taking the public footpath off left and turning left at the road. Bear right signposted Bettenham, keeping ahead past Bettenham Manor and as the road swings off right, keep ahead along the track leading to Sissinghurst Castle.

SISSINGHURST CASTLE. Although there is no mention of Sissinghurst in the Domesday Book, the name was recorded as early as 1180 with the mention of Stephen de Saxingherste and descendants of his family who held the manor in 1235. The manor was moated and three arms of the moat can still be seen, two of them water-filled, while the third arm has become a grass walk. The fourth arm was probably obliterated when Sir John Baker, Chancellor of the Exchequer to Queen Mary I, erected a red-brick mansion in 1535. Speculation has it that his son and heir Sir Richard Baker demolished the whole of the building save for the western entrance range, which still survives today, and built the tower and courtyard house some thirty years later. When the fourth John Baker died in 1661 he left a widow and four daughters and the estate was divided between them. But when the daughters each married holders of estates in other parts of the country, Sissinghurst was held by their mother and, following her death, her in-laws and their offspring. By the mid-eighteenth century its condition had deteriorated to "a house in ruins" and in 1756 was used as a prison during the Seven Years War, holding French prisoners-of-war until hostilities finished in 1763. It was then the title 'Castle' was given to Sissinghurst. In 1800 it was further destroyed, then used

The gazebo, Sissinghurst Castle.

The tower, Sissinghurst Castle, built by Sir Richard Baker in the 16th century.

The gazebo, boathouse and tower, Sissinghurst Castle.

as the village workhouse until 1855. It then became farm buildings, part of it being lived in by labourers who worked the land until Vita Sackville-West, a direct descendant of the Bakers and her husband Harold Nicholson, acquired it and lavished affection and hard work on its restoration. The gardens are their creation. Together they planned and planted an extraordinary garden in the grounds of the ruined mansion that amounted to nothing more than odd little buildings scattered about the site. It was on this plan that the garden was laid out, each part conceived to be self-contained, but each linked to the other parts by walks and vistas. They include a rose garden, a cottage garden - with an assortment of red, orange and yellow flowers - a herb garden, the White Garden - where lovely old roses are massed with other white and silvery flowers - and the lime walk, which in springtime is carpeted with flowers.

Vita Sackville-West died at Sissinghurst in June 1962 and Harold Nicholson died there in May 1968. Their son, on inheriting the castle, transformed the south wing of the entrance range into self-contained accommodation for his family, making over the castle and farmlands to the National Trust in 1967.

(National Trust Property. Open May-October. Admission charge)

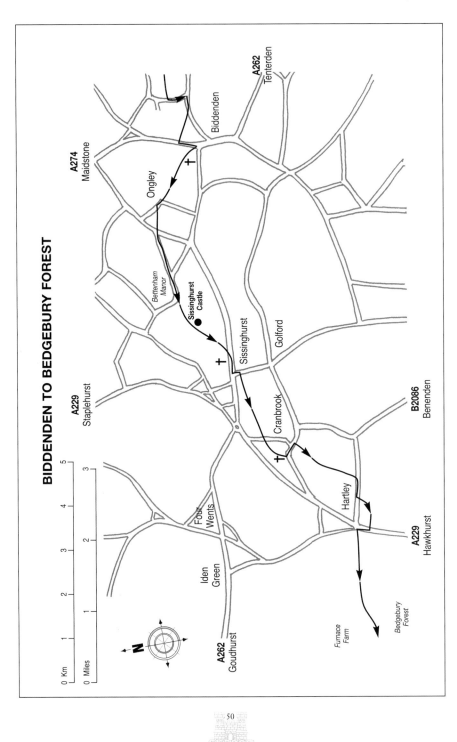

BIDDENDEN TO BEDGEBURY FOREST

Sissinghurst to Scotney Castle

Although only a relatively short section, it passes through the delightfully interesting Cranbrook, crosses the northern tip of the lovely Bedgebury Forest, skirts the idyllic setting of Bedgebury Park School and visits the little village of Kilndown. From here it is a very pleasant stretch through Kilndown Wood to the parkland surrounding Scotney castle.

Route: Leave the castle along a good track to the right of the car park, continuing along the edge of the woods where the path now becomes another good track as far as the road, where turn left at the public footpath signpost, following the path through the orchard. Bear right to the end of the wood, turning left across a bridge to continue ahead along the lane which leads onto the A262 just east of Sissinghurst village. (1.25 miles/2km)

SISSINGHURST VILLAGE. Originally called Milkhouse Street, this was once a prominent weaving centre when Kent's cloth industry developed in the fifteenth century. Among the attractive white weather-boarded cottages is the sixteenth century Sissinghurst Court, with a delightful garden. The village has a modern church, an old forge, a farm with a lake and a white windmill, but in truth the village is completely overshadowed by the castle a mile away.

Route: Turn left at Chapel Lane, the Benenden road, opposite the Bull Inn, and right at the public footpath signpost, keeping ahead at the cross-tracks to the lane, which cross straight over then down to the entrance to the wood. Follow the path through the wood to meet a track which skirts the southern boundary of Old Wilsley. Cross straight over at the B2189, meeting another path just above the church at Cranbrook. (1.75 miles/2.8km)

CRANBROOK. Set on a hill high above the Weald, here is a small town full of old wooden houses with a past running back 500 years to the days when rich Flemish merchants settled here. One of the tallest smock windmills in England stands just outside the town. Set on a tall brick base it was built by Henry Dobell in 1814 and rises to a height of 72 feet (22m). When he went bankrupt in 1819 he was forced to hand the mill over to a "union" of his creditors, hence its name Union Mill. It was restored in the 1950s and is still in full working order.

The church of St Dunstan was rebuilt by the Flemish merchants in 1430, leaving the old porch of 1291 with its vaulted roof meeting at a head encircled in foliage. The porch has a magnificent oak door about 6 feet wide and over the porch is a room in which martyrs were held captive. It was given the name Baker's Hole, because during the reign of Mary I protestants were tortured there before being burned at the stake. During the Napoleonic Wars French prisoners were also held in this room. The windows of the church are rich with colour and on the west wall, either side of the tower doorway, are two sculptures; one has portraits of two heroes of the South African war and the other is a relief by Hamo Thorneycroft of his friend Thomas Webster, who used to drive down the street in a donkey chaise.

The nave has a fine modern roof with slender shafts resting on stone heads, a queer seventeenth century baptistery, a handsome brass lectern, the brass of a mother and her little child and four enormous bosses fixed by the doorway to the tower. They used to be in the chancel roof and are deeply carved in oak.

Cranbrook School was chartered by Elizabeth I in 1574 and she really did sleep at the George Hotel. It is said that the king of England stayed there in 1299, in which case it dates back over 700 years. Close by the inn is Providence Chapel, built in 1828 and given a seven-sided wooden façade, specially treated to appear as stone.

Scotney Castle built between 1837 - 43 but it is the gardens which principally attract the visitors.

Route: Turn left out of the churchyard, past the George Hotel, turning right at The Tanyard just before the road off left, following the path beyond the car park to a cycle track where turn right. At Bramley Drive turn right following the track round left, ignoring the turn off right to Mount Ephraim Farm. Where the track splits take the right fork along a cinder track and where this peters out, follow the well-trodden path, bearing right at the open field. Fork right through kissing gate into Woodland Trust, keeping ahead to the road. At the road turn right and just beyond the entrance to Hartley Lands Farm Fishery on the right turn left at the public footpath signpost, heading diagonally right across the field. At the A229 in Hartley turn right, and at the point where the B2085 forks off left, turn left along a bridleway (Bishops Lane) which eventually crosses the bed of the old railway. Where the track splits take the left fork, keeping ahead to Furnace Farm. At the track immediately before the house, turn left towards the northern outskirts of Bedgebury Forest, ignoring track 97 off right but turning right onto the next bridleway. Follow the bridleway through the forest to the point where it turns off left and about 30 yards (28m) further on turn right at blue waymarker, emerging at drive to last oasthouse. Turn left through gate, heading diagonally right across field to stile. Head down left towards lake, offering a glorious panoramic view, following path along the edge of the lake and through the woods then along the left edge of the field to the road at Bedgebury Cross. Turn left at the road and in 50 yards (46m) right along the lane to Kilndown, turning off left to the church. (6 miles/9.6km)

KILNDOWN. Here is a nineteenth century church unlike any other in Kent. Built of sandstone, Christ Church was started in 1839 by Viscount Beresford of nearby Bedgebury Park, but in 1840 his stepson Alexander Beresford-Hope took over the project, turning the interior into a riot of colour. The walls were painted with stencilled patterns in red, blue and gold and the large pulpit, screen and font were painted too. Damp has penetrated the sandstone walls and the colours have diminished, but the font, screen and pulpit still retain their brilliant colouring. The stained-glass windows, created in Germany, are also in deep colours. Both the Viscount and his stepson are buried in the churchyard.

Route: Right out of the church and left at the public footpath signpost to Scotney Estate by the telephone box, following the track through Kilndown Wood. Once the path merges into a more definite track, follow the green waymarkers, looking for the footpath off right, through the grounds of Scotney Castle. At the approach to the castle turn right by the white gate (1 mile/1.6km)

SCOTNEY CASTLE. Though now in Kent, Scotney was formerly in Sussex, until the boundary was changed in 1897.

The earliest recorded possessor of the manor was Lambert de Scoteni in 1137, son or grandson of Walter Fitz Lambert, Lord of Crowhurst, Sussex in the Domesday Book. He held Scotney under the barony of Leeds Castle, near Maidstone, and it is possible that the site of his residency is represented by the smaller of the two islands enclosed by the present moat. In 1259 Walter de Scoteni is said to have been hanged at Winchester on suspicion of murder, and either as a result of this or the ensuing "Baron's War", the de Scoteni's disappear from the history of Scotney and the manor seems to have reverted to the Crown.

Early in 1310 is the next time Scotney comes into prominence, when the widow of John de Grofhurst married John de Ashburnham and their son Roger de Ashburnham succeeded to lands in "Courthope Scotney and Apdale" in right of his mother. In 1378 Ashburnham built Scotney Castle, not as a fortress but a fortified house, rectangular in shape, with four corner towers and a gatehouse strengthening the surrounding curtain wall enclosing a court. Only the Ashburnham Tower at the south corner survives intact, but the emplacements of the other three still exist and the four angle piers of the gatehouse still flank the entrance. The inner space is bisected by a range of buildings running north-west to south-east forming a forecourt towards the entrance and the garden, now called the bowling green, to the east. There is evidence that this range consisted of the usual hall of a manor house, with its entrance, facing the gatehouse, as the impost of the hall's front doorway and the arch of its rear doorway can still be seen. Only the southern half of this range survives, refaced and remodelled in the seventeenth century, with its south wing represented by the Elizabethan brick house adjoining the tower. In the south face of this, east of the tower, the fourteenth century curtain wall remains intact, with a little contemporary doorway.

Like other castles of its period, the principal defence was a wide moat, the supply of water for which dictated the site. The Scotney moat, or lake, contains two islands, of which the larger and more easterly carries the castle and is approached by way of the smaller (on which the boat house now stands). To make the moat, the River Bewl was diverted into a straight channel, contrasting with its sinuous course elsewhere, by a dam built alongside it for 300 yards connecting with higher ground at either end. A tributary stream, the Sweetbourne, here joined the Bewl, but at a level sufficiently above it to feed the moat and bring its surface some 8 feet above the normal level of the river into which the outflow falls at the eastern end. From the north the castle is closely overlooked from higher ground whereas in the south the river forms an outer defence.

After his death in 1392 Scotney was left to Ashburnham's widow and his son William, who died without issue in 1418, when the estate was sold to

Archbishop Chichele who gave it to his niece and her husband Thomas Darell of Ashford. Scotney remained in the Darell family for the next 350 years.

The south wing, adjoining the tower, was reconstructed about 1580, partly in brick and contained a fine oak staircase. As the Darell's were Catholics, incorporated into the building of the staircase were several secret hiding places in which their priests could be concealed during England's fight for freedom against Catholicism. One such priest, Father Blount, with his servant Bray, remained hidden for a week while the Darell's were out of the castle and it was occupied by their enemies. William Darell rebuilt much of the house around 1630. The east range, of which the fourteenth century hall had formed part, was refaced or reconstructed and although now a ruin, the walls largely remain, still incorporating some medieval masonry. Other parts of the old castle were probably demolished. The northern half was never built, probably because of William Darell's death in 1639 and then the outbreak of the Civil War.

In 1726 Georgian alterations were made with the little glazed cupola and conical roof surmounting the tower and in 1778 the Darell ownership came to an end when Edward Hussey bought the castle, acquiring other lands belonging to the Darell estate during the next ten years.

The New Castle was built to the designs of Anthony Salvin between February 1837 and May 1843 and the Old Castle was used in connection with the garden landscape, parts demolished to retain features of interest and increase the romantic character of the scenic gardens. The estate remained in the Hussey family until 1970 when it was bequeathed to the National Trust. Today it is the gardens which principally attract the visitor.

(National Trust Property. Open April-October. Admission charge.)

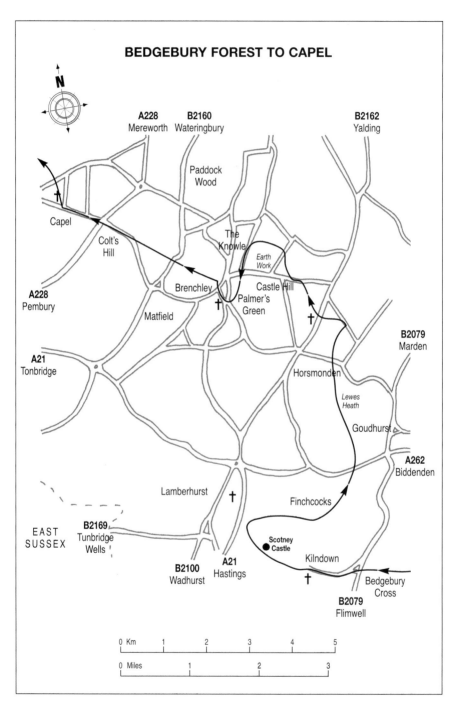

BEDGEBURY FOREST TO CAPEL

N

A228 **B2160**
Mereworth Wateringbury

B2162
Yalding

Paddock
Wood

Capel

Colt's
Hill

The
Knowle

*Earth
Work*

Brenchley

Castle Hill

Palmer's
Green

A228
Pembury

Matfield

B2079
Marden

A21
Tonbridge

Horsmonden

*Lewes
Heath*

Goudhurst

A262
Biddenden

Lamberhurst

Finchcocks

B2169
Tunbridge
Wells

**EAST
SUSSEX**

Scotney
Castle

Kilndown

Bedgebury
Cross

B2100
Wadhurst

A21
Hastings

B2079
Flimwell

0 Km   1   2   3   4   5

0 Miles   1   2   3

Scotney Castle to Castle Hill

The route from Scotney Castle follows the Teise valley to the impressive Finchcocks, and from there crosses the fine parkland of Rectory Park to Lewes Heath. Passing through the orchards surrounding Horsmonden we follow more orchards to the indistinct earthworks at Castle Hill on the outskirts of Brenchley.

Route: Retrace steps back to the bridge and turn sharp right in the direction of the yellow waymarker. Cross the approach road to the castle (not an official right of way for walkers from the castle) and continue into the woods, following the yellow waymarkers to a T-junction. Turn left here and over a stile (signposted Lamberhurst) where there is a panoramic view ahead. Turn left at the concrete track and right immediately before the bridge.

LAMBERHURST. Although our route does not visit this attractive village, it was once an important iron-producing centre where in 1710 the railings of St Paul's Cathedral were wrought. Its church of St Mary can be seen to the left of the A21. With its fourteenth century arches and windows, the church stands in a lovely setting, with a yew near the door as old as any part of it. Its trunk, 25 feet round, was here when Edward I visited in the last year of the thirteenth century. The old rood loft steps are still here, entered by a Tudor doorway, and the crude timbers of the roof are original. Inside is an ancient stone bench by the altar and the remains of a three-decker pulpit over 300 years old. On the lower deck sat the priest, on the middle deck was the reading desk and the upper deck was the pulpit. Today the lower deck is gone, but it is a finely carved masterpiece for all that.

Route: Follow the path alongside the A21, turning off right at the public footpath signpost, across the field to a stile leading back into the Scotney Estate. Keep ahead in the direction of the yellow waymarkers with Finchcocks the large house on the sky line. Continue ahead along the right edge of the hop field, bearing left across two paddocks before crossing the stile to the lane. Left here and over the stile right, crossing the field to the wood. Immediately after leaving the wood turn off left over a stile behind the oak tree and immediately over another stile into the adjoining field. Cross this field diagonally left to another stile in the far right corner, down a flight of steps to turn left at the footpath. Keep ahead past the houses then over a stile by the metal gate, turning right immediately afterwards, over another stile and crossing the field with Finchcocks on the left. Over another stile and ahead along the approach road to Finchcocks (turning left to visit the house.) (2.5 miles/4km)

FINCHCOCKS. This is a fine early Georgian manor, noted for its outstanding brickwork and front elevation, attributed to Thomas Archer. The house is named after the family who lived on the site in the thirteenth century, although the present house was built in 1725. Despite having changed hands many times it has suffered remarkably little alteration and retains most of its original features. In 1970 the manor was acquired by Richard Burnett, leading exponent of the period piano, and it now houses his magnificent collection of over one hundred historical keyboard instruments: chamber organs, virginals, harpsichords, clavichords as well as a wide range of early pianos - about forty of which are fully restored to concert condition. There are also a number of barrel organs, musical boxes and other mechanical instruments, most of which can be seen and heard whenever the house is open. There is also a collection of musical pictures, prints and an exhibition on the theme of eighteenth century Pleasure Gardens.

The gardens have been fully restored with wide lawns, mature shrub borders, orchard and a beautiful walled garden which is used for outside events. Informal recitals by professional musicians whenever the house is open.

Privately owned. Open on Sundays April-September, Bank Holiday Mondays, and Wednesdays and Thursdays in August, 1400-1800 (gardens from 1230). Admission Charge. Teas available.

Route: Continue along approach road, forking left where road splits. Turn right at A262 to Green Cross Inn, where turn off left at public footpath signpost opposite. Over stile right to continue left alongside the edge of the field, following boundary round to stile by metal gate leading onto lane. Turn off left to Crowbourne Oast and at the lane turn left then left again at the fork onto cycle route 18. Turn left at the T-junction, following the road round left at Trottenden Farm, crossing the River Teise and keeping straight ahead at the crossroads. Turn right over stile opposite the road into Rectory Park on the High Weald Landscape Trail. At the road keep ahead into Horsmonden, another ironworking centre along with cloth making. Turn right at the road and left at the track to Bassetts Farm, keeping ahead through the orchard and passing through an arch in the leylandii hedge and ahead through gate. Follow the path across the field to road where turn left and left again in 50 yards (46m) at the public footpath signpost. Follow the path through the orchard, keeping to the right of the high hedge, to All Saints Catholic church at the road. Turn off left at the public footpath signpost just beyond the church, passing under the disused railway then along a track through Swigs Hole Farm. Keep ahead through the orchard as the main track swings off right, turning right before bearing left onto track to the road. Turn left at the road, and where the road leads off left to Horsmonden, turn right at the public footpath signpost, following the path left and then round right. Turn off left in about 50 yards (46m) along a green path, looking for a gap in the hedge where five steps lead onto the road, which cross to reach the earthworks at Castle Hill. (6.5 miles/10.5km)

Scotney Castle Manor House.

CASTLE HILL. Commonly known as Brenchley or Knowle Castle, it consists of a double ring of defensive earthworks and stands about 1 mile (1.6km) north-east of Brenchley.

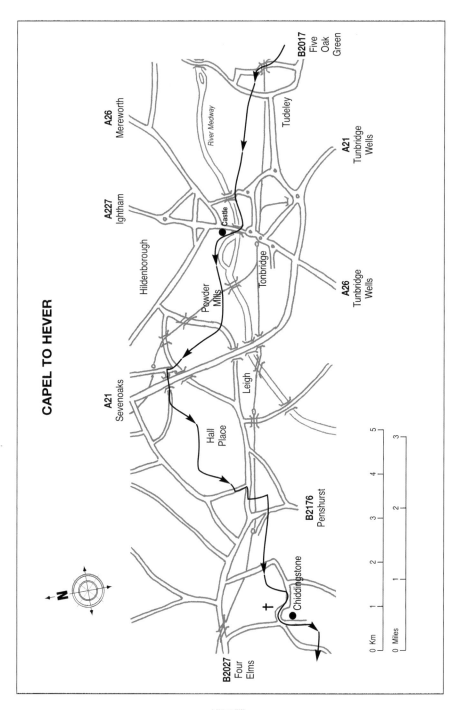

CAPEL TO HEVER

B2017 Five Oak Green
A26 Mereworth
River Medway
Tudeley
A21 Tunbridge Wells
A227 Ightham
Castle
Tonbridge
A26 Tunbridge Wells
Hildenborough
Powder Mlls
A21 Sevenoaks
Leigh
Hall Place
B2176 Penshurst
Chiddingstone
B2027 Four Elms

N

0 Km 1 2 3 4 5
0 Miles 1 2 3

Castle Hill to Tonbridge

Another relatively short section, passing through the quaint centre of Brenchley, more synonymous orchards and the fascinating wall paintings in the church at Capel. Still more orchards bring us to the Medway and the Wealdway which follow its bank to the majestic towers of Tonbridge castle.

Route: Follow the yellow waymarkers round the right edge of the field to the stile by the cattle pens at Knowle Lodge. Over the stile and along track to road, where turn left. At the T-junction cross to a stile a little to the left of the houses, following a well signposted path around the edge of an orchard then along a delightful enclosed path (ignoring the left fork) to the road. (1.25 miles/2km).

BRENCHLEY. This ancient hilltop village has a mixture of half-timbered Tudor cottages, weather-boarded houses and buildings with tiled facades, many of which are listed, as well as shops and pubs, all on a fine square and tiny green where the village pound once stood. Houses of particular interest are the Old Vicarage - dated 1320, Butchers Shop, Church House, Brenchley Manor (Old Parsonage) and Brattles Grange.

All Saints church, dating from the thirteenth century, is approached by a grand avenue of 350-year-old trimmed yew trees. It has had several alterations and additions through the centuries, but contains some interesting tombs and its treasure, the exquisitely carved rood screen dating from 1536. The hammerbeam roof of the chancel with splendid angels supporting it may well be work by the same craftsmen and our four national saints look down from one of the chancel windows. Much of the church remains as it was in 1233, when the arches and door were built, but the porch is fourteenth century. There are two brasses: one to Thomas Roberts with three wives and eleven children and another of 1450 to an unknown merchant and his wife.

The Old Palace nearby was once used by the Archbishops of Canterbury and has been restored in an attempt to recapture the Tudor, half-timbered original. Another important building is the early seventeenth century Old Workhouse, now one of the finest group of cottages in Kent.

Route: From the church turn up left, passing the Bull Inn and the Rose and Crown public house before forking right and keeping ahead at the footpath at the T-junction. Follow the well-directed, well-trodden path through the orchard, keeping generally in the same direction to the road, which cross straight over. Continue along a track, bearing right by the twin oast and right again along an enclosed path, turning right at the T-junction to Gedges Farm, then left at the track to the road. Right at the road, following it round left past Crittenden and straight over the road at Colt's Hill. Continue past Dovecote Inn to the church at Capel. (4 miles/6.4km)

CAPEL. The parish church here is dedicated to St Thomas a Becket and once belonged to the Knights Templar. Built in the twelfth century it was partially rebuilt in the seventeenth century after a fire caused by lightning. Some interesting thirteenth century wall paintings portraying Christ's death and resurrection have survived.

Route: Leave via the path from the back of the churchyard, crossing the field and then following the field edge round right, over stile and through copse, emerging at the road by the George and Dragon public house, crossing straight over and passing just to the right of a pylon. Under the power lines, following the field edge down to the railway, turning left alongside the railway embankment to the road. Turn right under the railway and where the road swings off right keep ahead at the public footpath, following the path through an orchard, gently edging right until an open field appears on the left. Drop down then back up through the hedge to continue alongside the right edge of this field to the road at Tudeley Hale. Cross straight over keeping in a straight direction to the lane where turn left then right at the T-junction onto a good track past The Postern, to the road. Cross straight over to continue along the bank of the River Medway, past the lock, crossing the bridge over the river to Tonbridge Castle. (3.75 miles/6km)

TONBRIDGE. Here is a market town on the upper reaches of the River Medway, which began developing as early as the Iron Age. It has continued to prosper, thanks to its geographical position, for when, in the eighteenth century, the Medway was made navigable as far up as the town local produce was brought here to be shipped out. It was also on the main route to the south coast and so became a staging post for mail coaches. Finally, the coming of the railway in 1842 ensured its continuing importance with even easier access to London.

The church of St Peter & St Paul dates from the twelfth century but contains later work and many notable monuments. Two fire hooks can be seen in the church porch; used for dragging thatch off burning houses, they are a reminder of the time when the porch was used as a fire station and housed a fire engine. Three windows in the nave are Norman and the north arcade is thirteenth century, but the foundations of the wall seen through these arches were old when the arches were built, for they are Saxon. By the altar lie two stone figures in separate niches in the wall. One is Sir Anthony Denton and his 'dear

Tonbridge Castle. The gatehouse was built around 1300 by Richard de Clare, the rest of the castle was demolished in 1793.

and doleful' wife. On the north wall is a sculpture by *Ronbillae* made in 1753.

Tonbridge School was founded as a Free Grammar School in 1553 by Sir Andrew Judd, who became Lord Mayor of London. The original schoolhouse was destroyed when the school became a private boarding establishment in 1864 and has been completely rebuilt.

The chapel, built in rich red brick is well lighted and has a black and white hammer-beam roof 150 feet long. On the walls are an Italian fresco of the Last Supper, two wood carvings and an attractive group of painted sculptures. It is a copy from the tomb of Sir Andrew Judd, founder of the school, who lies in Bishopsgate in London. But it is for the glass that the chapel will perhaps be best remembered.

A fort was built on what is now Castle Hill as long ago as the Iron Age to defend the ford which offered an easy crossing of the Medway. In the eleventh century the Normans recognised its strategic importance, so overlooking the Medway they built a stronghold. Richard Fitzgilbert built the castle surrounded by a moat fed from the river on a site covering an acre and rising 100 feet above the river. The castle has four immense round towers and a gateway of great strength.

During 1088 the castle held out against William Rufus, but Fitzgilbert was wounded during the siege and the castle surrendered. He died in Normandy in 1091. In 1264 Gilbert de Clare set out from here to lead de Montfort's army at Lewes, but he quarrelled with de Montfort and joined the King's side at Evesham the following year, later marrying Prince Edward's daughter. Around 1300 Richard de Clare built the gatehouse, which still stands today. In 1314 de Clare's only son, Gilbert, was killed at Bannockburn and Tonbridge passed to his sisters. One of these married Hugh de Audley, who rebelled against Edward and consequently forfeited his right to the castle. Edward III restored it to Audley and on his death it passed to his daughter Margaret, who married Lord Stafford, a great soldier who commanded at Crecy in 1346. One of the Staffords was killed fighting for Henry IV at Shrewsbury in 1403 and later Staffords, Dukes of Buckingham, also met violent deaths. One died at Northampton in 1460, another at St Albans in 1461 and Henry, the 2nd Duke, was executed in Salisbury by Richard III. His son Edward, restored to the title, became High Constable of England but, falling foul of Cardinal Wolsley, was accused of treason, tried and beheaded in 1520.

Held for Parliament during the Civil War the castle was not demolished until 1793, when it was bought by Thomas Hooker of Peckham who constructed the present Gothic bulding, now used as municipal offices, next to the gatehouse. The bailey is a garden and only a small piece of the wall remains.

Open daily 9-5. Admission charge.

View of Hever Castle and topiary.

Hever Castle's attractive 'village' behind the Castle.

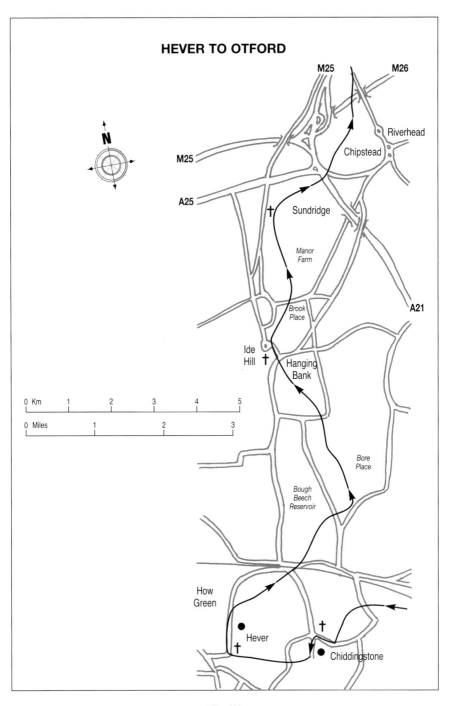

HEVER TO OTFORD

N

M25

M26

Riverhead

M25

Chipstead

A25

✝ Sundridge

Manor Farm

Brook Place

A21

Ide Hill ✝

Hanging Bank

Bore Place

0 Km   1   2   3   4   5

0 Miles   1   2   3

Bough Beech Reservoir

How Green

● ✝ Hever

✝ ● Chiddingstone

Tonbridge to Hever Castle

The route out of Tonbridge follows the pleasant Eden Valley Walk before turning off to Powder Mills, then follows a delightful stretch past Hall Place. Then follows some pleasant country walking before hitting the track which leads into the National Trust village of Chiddingstone. Chiddingstone Castle is always visible as we follow the road round to its entrance and from there we rejoin the Eden Valley Way to Hever church and the entrance to its famous castle.

Route: From the castle join the Eden Valley Walk, heading west under the railway and forking right. At the bridge fork right again to the lake, keeping ahead to the oasthouse at Powder Mills. Turn left at the road and in 130 yards (119m) right at the public footpath signpost by The Hutchings, following the path to the stile left of the large white house. After passing the white house, turn off left down an earth track, following it round left but turning right over a stile just before the track turns right, following the path to the road. Left at the road and right signposted Hildenborough Station, turning off left down Lower Street, signposted to Weald and under the A21. Turn left at the public footpath signpost, heading diagonally right across the field, crossing the stream and heading into the woods. Leave the woods down an earth track, turning right at the waymarker and cross the bridge with a clapper stile. Then turn right at the metal kissing gate in just a few steps, continuing along a long, straight enclosed path, eventually offering a nice view over to the left of Hall Place and its lake. Devey built the mansion in the Tudor style between 1871-6 for Samuel Morley M.P. At the end of the wood, turn left to Price's Farm and follow the driveway as far as the wood, where turn right at the marker post, following the path as it skirts the wood to the road. Turn left at the road and right at the T-junction, turning left again at the next public footpath signpost, crossing the railway and meeting at a cross-tracks on the outskirts of more woods. Turn right here and right at the road, turning left at the public footpath signpost, following the track round right, over the stream then left through the metal gate with the yellow waymarker. At the cross-tracks keep ahead to the left of the hedge, crossing the stile to the left of the house. Cross straight over at road and at the drive turn left, through the gate to continue along a path over the river to the road. Turn right here into Chiddingstone. (9 miles/14.5km)

CHIDDINGSTONE. The village is owned by the National Trust. Most of the houses are sixteenth and seventeenth century; the Old Rectory is eighteenth century and the pargetted Castle Inn is dated 1637. The thirteenth century church of St Mary the Virgin has a variety of styles and part of it was rebuilt after a fire in 1625. Two cast iron slabs dated 1601 and 1715 can be seen in the floor.

Route: Follow the road round right out of the village, over the bridge to the cross-roads, where turn left to Hill Hoath. The entrance to Chiddingstone Castle is off to the left. (0.75 mile/1.2km)

CHIDDINGSTONE CASTLE. The seventeenth century manor house of the Streatfields, known as High Street House, was remodelled into a castellated mansion in the early nineteenth century by Henry Kendall. On display are collections of Ancient Egyptian relics, Japanese weapons and material relating to the Royal House of Stuart, gathered by Denys Eyre Bowen, who lived at Chiddingstone Castle from 1955 until his death in 1977. The lake is a major feature of the park.

(Privately owned. Open April-October daily (except Monday) 1400-1730 Saturday/Sunday and Bank Holidays 1130-1730. Admission charge)

Route: Follow the road past the castle to Hill Hoath. Once the road swings right, continue along the right fork and keep right as the path splits again. Where the footpath and bridleway split fork right onto footpath to cross a stream before turning left to the road. Cross straight over and keep ahead on the Eden Valley Way to Hever church. (2 miles/3.2km)

Chiddingstone Castle, a 17th century manor house remodelled into a castellated mansion in the early 19th century.

HEVER. A castle, a church and an inn, with one or two houses and the odd farm set in some of the loveliest scenery in Kent. The church of St Peter stands at the castle gates, with its fourteenth century tower and graceful spire, one of the finest shingled spires in the county, rising to 100 feet. Most of the church is between 500 and 600 years old, with the original timbers of its barrel roof and a fine old Jacobean pulpit. The curious lectern and iron screens were made by a rector and the painting of Christ, in the chancel, is by Ruben Sayers. There are three memorials in brass; Margaret Cheyne, with two lovely angels at her head and a small dog at her feet, dated 1419. Mounted on a windowsill is a brass of William Todde, a teacher of history before the Spanish Armada, but the most famous of all is that of Thomas Bullen of 1538. The proud owner of Hever Castle he was the father of Anne Boleyn and she spent her blissful childhood here. Following her death and that of her brother her father became a broken man. Here is his final resting place, in a an old stone tomb, worn and battered with the passing of time.

Route: Turn right out of the churchyard, past the Henry VIII inn to the entrance to Hever Castle.

HEVER CASTLE. The first owners of Hever were a Norman family who built a fortified farmhouse, surrounded by a moat and approached by a wooden drawbridge, at the end of the thirteenth century. By the middle of the fourteenth century it was granted a licence to crenellate and when the de Cobham family took possession around 1380 they were granted permission to add more embattlements. During the next eighty years ownership of the castle changed six times and it was Sir Geoffrey Bullen, a Norfolkman who had been Lord Mayor of London, who purchased Hever in 1462. His grandson Thomas became owner in 1505 and held various posts at Court. It was inevitable that his two daughters would also go to Court and Mary, the youngest daughter, soon became lady-in-waiting to Queen Catherine and caught the eye of Henry VIII. After a period of amorous advances the King tired of Mary and instead turned his attention to Anne. Her father also benefited the royal affections, becoming Treasurer of the Household in 1522, was created a Knight of the Garter the following year and in 1525 was elevated to the peerage as Viscount Rochford. Four years later he rose still higher to become Earl of Wiltshire and Earl of Ormonde.

But Anne had no intention of becoming the King's mistress, insisting on becoming his Queen or nothing. But Henry was already married, to Catherine of Aragon, his Queen of eighteen years. She bore him a daughter, Mary, but no son, so the King convinced himself he had no alternative but to divorce Catherine and take another wife in order to ensure the male succession.

Hereby a complication. Such a divorce could only be arranged by the Pope, but as the Holy Roman Emperor was the powerful Charles V, King of Spain, King of Austria and ruler of the Hapsburg possessions in the Netherlands and the New World - and Catherine's nephew! - the Pope, who was in the French King's control, did not want to antagonize him, so he refused the request. Henry was furious, but a chink of hope appeared with the sudden death of the incorruptible Archbishop of Canterbury in 1532. The King appointed Thomas Cranmer, Archdeacon of Taunton, as the new Archbishop of Canterbury, who he knew he could manipulate to repudiate the Pope's jurisdiction and give the desired judgement in this affair. With immediate effect the Pope's authority was abolished and Henry VIII made himself Supreme Head of the Church of England and the breach with Rome was complete. Soon afterwards the monasteries were suppressed, the Book of Common Prayer was authorized and the Reformation was promoted.

In January 1533 Anne was already pregnant and in order that her baby "might be born legitimate", Henry and Anne were married in the same month by an Augustinian friar in a private chapel and she was crowned Queen on 1st June that same year. But the son he craved was a daughter and the following year Anne suffered a miscarriage. Two years later she delivered a stillborn son and then she suffered another miscarriage. Disappointment became impatience; rage turned to intolerance and the King was made to look ridiculous. He was determined to be rid of her, especially as by now he had fallen in love with her maid of honour, Jane Seymour. Because of her neglect by the King and her own flirtatious nature she attracted several other young men at the court and on 2nd May 1536 she was arrested and taken to the Tower of London on a charge of High Treason for adultery with four men, one of them her brother. All four men were found guilty and sentenced to death and Cranmer tried in vain to force her to declare that she had never been lawfully married to the King and that her three-year-old daughter was illegitimate. But she refused to do this and was tried on the 15th May and found guilty and was condemned to death by her own uncle, the Duke of Norfolk. She was beheaded four days later and on the same day Henry was granted a special licence to marry Jane Seymour. Her daughter grew up to become Elizabeth I, one of the great rulers of our nation.

Anne's parents continued to live at Hever and after their deaths the Crown took possession, but the King made little use of it except to grant it to Anne of Cleves, his fourth wife, in 1540, whom he had recently divorced, and in whose possession it remained until her death in 1557.

Mary Tudor was now on the throne, and when Hever once again reverted to the Crown she granted it to Sir Edward Waldegrave, who had been Head

Warden in the Tower of London at the time of Mary's imprisonment, in recognition of the kindness he had shown her. She made him Chancellor of the Duchy of Lancaster, but on her death he fell into disfavour with Elizabeth I and was sent to the Tower where he died in 1561.

From the late sixteenth century Hever fell from grace and at one time became a meeting place for smugglers. New owners came and went and in 1749 it came into the possession of the Meade Waldo family. By the end of the nineteenth century the castle was occupied by humble farmers and it was not until 1903, when the castle was rescued from an ignoble state by William Waldorf Astor, that it was once again restored to something like its former splendour.

Astor was the great grandson of John Jacob Astor who acquired great wealth by establishing a successful trading business in America, buying furs from the Indian trappers of the Great Lakes and exporting the pelts to the markets of the world. But William Waldorf Astor had a passionate love for Europe, possibly derived from his period as American Ambassador to Italy, and he settled in England in 1890, where he became a naturalized British subject. He was created a Peer of the Realm and lived at Hever until his death in 1919.

The estate then went to his younger son John Jacob Astor, who sought permanent domicile in France in 1962, passing it on to their eldest son Gavin. The entrance to the castle is its main feature and behind the drawbridge, leading into the courtyard, is a Norman arch extending the whole depth of the keep. This was defended by three strong wooden portcullises and two thick oak gates, barred and studded with iron bolts. The innermost gate contains a small door allowing access from the courtyard to the entrance and spiral stairway - to the boiler room and guardrooms. When the Astors took possession this small door was missing, but was eventually located at a nearby farm and repositioned. Of the three portcullises only two remain, the outer one believed to be the only genuine wooden portcullis still in working order in England today.

The projections surrounding and surmounting the entrance archway are later additions to the original castle, probably added during John de Cobham's time or by Sir Geoffrey Bullen. The wooden drawbridge is not the original, which was replaced by a brick bridge at the end of the eighteenth century when the castle became a farmhouse.

The original entrance under the archway was blocked up during the fifteenth century, and later that century living rooms inside the walls were added by the Bullens and a new entrance was constructed, leading off the courtyard. The Astors blocked these doors and constructed a new entrance in line with the archway, leading into the entrance hall.

Most of the windows were inserted by the Bullens in Henry VIII's time. The round tower at the north-west corner of the outer walls was added in 1567 and originally the moat extended right up to the castle walls, the small terrace not being built until the eighteenth century.

Guide to the Castle The floor of the Courtyard is paved with hard wearing ironstone quarried from Ide Hill in 1904 and the bronze sundial is by Henry Moore. The wine barrel is seventeenth century Burgundian and the cannons are thought to be sixteenth century Italian. Now pass through into...

The Entrance Hall, in which the wooden arch and beams are fifteenth century originals, houses two sixteenth century suits of armour from northern Italy. The postilion's boots decorated with fleur-de-lis and lettering in stringwork are French, from the seventeenth century while the oak panel carved with the four evangelists is fifteenth century Italian. The figures of the Foolish Virgin, of the Madonna, and of St Margaret rising from the dragon's body and holding a cross in her clasped hands are sixteenth century French. The cope and choir stall are sixteenth and seventeenth century Italian.

The oak panelling in the Drawing Room is inlaid with black bog-oak and holly. It is copied from the haunted room of Sizergh Castle, Cumbria, whose panelling is now in the Victoria and Albert Museum, and was made in 1905. The Inner Hall, formerly the kitchen, is now panelled from floor to ceiling with Italian walnut. In the mid-nineteenth century the north-east corner of the Inner Hall collapsed and had to be built up again, and at the same time the well was filled in. The staircase and gallery were copied from King's College, Cambridge, while the ceiling typifies sixteenth century work, incorporating the Tudor rose and a silver chandelier.

The bust of Henry VIII is carved in cannel coal and the sculpture of St Catherine is fifteenth century Flemish. The sixteenth century silvered clock, engraved with the Royal coat of arms, is a copy of the one given by Henry VIII to Anne Boleyn on the occasion of their marriage. The layette was made by a young Elizabeth I for the expected infant of her half-sister, Mary Tudor, who was married to Philip II of Spain. The mounted figure is of Joan of Arc which was carved in the fifteenth century. In the Dining Hall the fireplace of Clipsham stone from Rutland and the Bullen arms surmounting it were constructed in 1904. The heraldic emblazonments in the windows are also modern, and beneath the windows can be seen the place where knives were sharpened on the stone. The only original piece of stained glass that was found in the castle at the time of the restoration is now in the Minstrel's Gallery. The elaborate network of carving on the screen of the Minstrel's Gallery was completed in 1904.

One of the door locks belonged to Henry VIII and bears his coat of arms. He always carried it around with him and had it fastened onto the door of his bedroom. The other lock is a copy.

The pair of silver chairs are seventeenth century German, but the Spanish style chairs are modern. The three suits of armour belonged to Francis I of France (1515-1547). Henry II of France (1547-1559) and the three-quarter harness to the Duke of Parma, Governor of the Netherlands.

In the west wing the Library and Study are lined with panelling and bookcases made of sabicu, a naturally scented wood, hard as ebony, from South America. The carving of flowers, birds and leaves in the style of Grinling Gibbons enrich the cornices, pilasters, doors and mantelpiece. The design was taken from Magdalene College, Cambridge and the ceiling was inspired by one at Hampton Court. The floor is made up of Spanish mahogany laid on Swedish pine. The portrait of the first John Jacob Astor (1763-1848) is a copy of the one by the American artist Gilbert Stuart and there are bronzes by Sansovino, John Bologna and others.

In the Morning Room the fireplace bearing the initials 'H.W.' and the panelling were brought to Hever by Sir Henry Waldegrave from Sparrow's Hall, Ipswich. The iron fireback carries the arms, supporters and crest of Elizabeth I. The floor is made of Spanish mahogany laid on Swedish pine and part of the west wall is more than six feet thick.

The headdress was worked by Anne Boleyn, and of the furniture the chairs are Tudor turnwood and the silver table is Spanish belonging to the sixteenth century. The pair of large vases are K'ang His and the blue china is from Delft. In the gilt cabinet, designed by Goose, is a collection of ivories ranging in date from the fifteenth to the nineteenth century.

The Long Gallery on the second floor was built by the Bullen family and its panelling is original of Elizabethan date and is some of the finest still in situ in the country. In the oriel window are emblazoned the Tudor arms in modern painted glass, while in the other windows are the coats of arms of the owners of Hever from 1200 to 1903. The ceiling was plastered in sixteenth century style in 1904 to replace one of plain design. The silver chandeliers of Charles II design were made for the Astors in 1906.

The suits of armour are Spanish, Italian and German of the sixteenth century. The gilt and enamel inlaid helmet belonged to Boabdil, ruler of Granada and last of the Moors to be driven out of Spain by the Christians Ferdinand and Isabella, parents of Catherine of Aragon, in 1492 - the year that Christopher

Columbus sailed from Spain to discover America.

The carved stone and marble figures are French, Italian and Flemish ranging from the thirteenth to the eighteenth centuries.

In the first cabinet the forearm from a silver figure of 'Victory' was presented by the Emperor Varus to the 6th Roman Legion, which was in England in AD150. The arm was dug up near Rochdale in 1790. The gold christening bowl was given by the 1st Viscount Astor of Hever Castle to his grandson Gavin in 1918.

The portrait of Anne Boleyn is by an unknown artist, but the sedan chair, now containing seventeenth century Venetian glass ornaments, was once the property of Cardinal Richelieu, the Minister of Louis XIII and 'the builder of France'. The bed head and posts belonged to Anne Boleyn. The coffer carved with the initials of Sir Thomas Bullen and his wife Elizabeth was probably made at Hever Castle to commemorate his elevation to the peerage as Viscount Rochford in 1525. The chairs belong to the Jacobean and William and Mary periods.

The large casket of rock crystal is sixteenth century Venetian workmanship. It was presented by Pope Clement VIII to Marie of Medici, second wife of Henry IV of France and Navarre, on the occasion of the birth of Louis XIII at Fontainebleau in 1601, and contained swaddling clothes which the Pope himself had blessed. The Papal Bull printed in old Latin is one of the originals distributed by the Medici Pope Clement VII refusing Henry VIII's divorce from Catherine of Aragon. On the flag are the arms of the Medicis, wealthy sixteenth century rulers of Florence.

In the second cabinet the crystal and enamel reliquary which was intended to contain a relic of St Luke's forearm was made for Queen Isabella of Castile at the end of the fifteenth century. The caskets and other crystals range in date from the fifteenth to nineteenth centuries. The clocks are German of the seventeenth century. The toilet articles are reputed to have belonged to Elizabeth I.

In The Keep the two main rooms are now known as the Council Chamber and the Armoury, from which some narrow stone stairs lead out onto the battlements. This is approached by a stone-roofed hooded porch, the only one still in existence in an English domestic dwelling. In the Armoury is a curious little secret room built into the thickness of the walls - a hiding place built long before the Civil War when hunted priests frequently hid and Royalists evaded discovery by the Parliamentarians. The pair of organ cheeks carved in limewood are fifteenth century Flemish and the scene of the Crucifixion was carved in ivory by Jaillot, sculptor to Louis XIV in 1690. The silver-gilt richly enamelled cross is fifteenth century Florentine, and the crook with Lion of St Mark is fifteenth century Italian. The throne belonged to Doge Pietro Lando, sixteenth century ruler of Venice and defender of the city against the Turks, whom he defeated in 1559; carved on the arms are the lions of St Mark. In the glass cabinet, the reliquaries and monstrance are of the fourteenth and fifteenth centuries. The sixteenth century biretta belonged to the Venetian Doge and the bishops' mitres date from the thirteenth century. The other Roman Catholic vestments are Italian sixteenth and seventeenth century.

The various carved figures of saints are sixteenth century; the bust of Christ is by Verrocchio and the carved wooden figure of an ecclesiastic is late twelfth century French. The small sculpture of St Francis is fourteenth century Florentine while the alabaster figure of the Madonna is sixteenth century Flemish.

Two counterweights for the portcullis hang on chains from the armoury above and in the Armoury, also known as the Torture Chamber, a collection of medieval instruments of torture, discipline and execution is on display. These were bought by Mr Astor from the Christian Hammer Museum, Stockholm, at the beginning of last century.

Exit to the Courtyard for access to the Gardens.

Within four years of William Waldorf Astor taking possession of Hever he had converted 60 acres into modest gardens, including a 30-acre lake, flower beds typical of those which might have existed in the time of Henry VIII and Anne Boleyn, a maze planted with more than one thousand yew trees and other topiary work also cut out of yew trees. There were little paved courts, rose gardens and even a bowling green, all surrounded by an outer moat. Beyond the outer moat and at a discreet distance from the castle all manner of walks, avenues and gardens were formed. To the south of the castle was an imposing Rhododendron Walk at the far end of which the South Garden was made and the Golden Stairs were built. Close by the South Garden is Sunday Walk with its running stream, waterfalls, rockeries, bamboo and shrub plantations. From here Anne Boleyn's Walk stretches away to Splashwater where it connects with the Smugglers' Way.

By the shore of the lake a huge loggia with colonnaded piazza was built, with a huge fountain and figures carved by the sculptor Frith. Behind the piazza an Italian Garden complete with pergola, Roman bath, grottoes and marble pavements was laid out, designed to accommodate the figures Mr Astor had collected during his service as American Minister in Rome.

Privately owned. Open daily March-November 1100-1800. Admission charge.

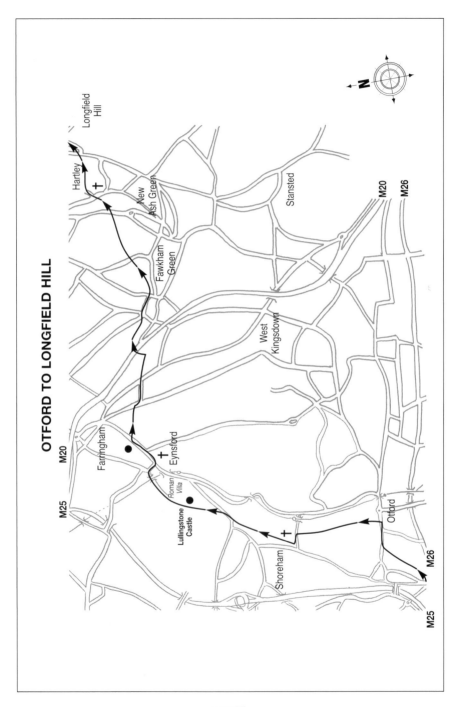

OTFORD TO LONGFIELD HILL

Ꞩever to Lullingstone Castle

Hever is as far west as the route takes us and we now have to work our way up to the North Downs on another long stretch between castles. En route is Bough Beech Reservoir, of which there are commanding views as we skirt Hanging Bank on the approach to Ide Hill, and then on to Sundridge, an important place long before the Norman Conquest. The seemingly complicated intersection of the A25/M25/A21 is negotiated with relative ease before joining the Darent Valley Path at Chipstead and we follow it beyond the outskirts of Otford to the delightful village of Shoreham. The river is never far from view from here to Lullingstone.

Route: Turn right out of the castle, following the road to How Green. Turn right at the public footpath signpost, over the stile and across the golf course, turning left over the stream and keeping to the right edge of the golf course. Turn right over the stile at the waymarker, following the edge of the field and turning left at the lane to the B2027, which cross by The Wheatsheaf, turning right then left in 50 yards (46m) to cross the railway. Follow the well-defined path over two stiles to another stile just

Lullingstone Castle gatehouse. Beyond was once a moat and then a further gatehouse giving entrance to the manor house.

below the dam wall of Bough Beech Reservoir, then cross the field diagonally right and over the approach road to the Sailing Club. Cross the next two fields separated by a ditch to a road, which cross, then over another field to a road where turn left. Keep ahead to Bore Place as the road swings off right, then the track bends first left then right to the road by Scollops Farm, where turn right a few steps before turning off left at the yellow waymarker, following the path across a bridge before continuing alongside the right edge of the next field, and then on to the tapered end of the field beyond. Keep straight across the next two fields, then along an enclosed path to a lane where turn right. Follow the road round Hanging Bank to the road, where turn left past the toilets and across the road beyond before turning right up to the picnic area. Carry on up the steps at the far end, taking the right fork up to a bench seat and on to the church at Ide Hill. (6 miles/9.6km)

IDE HILL.

A remote village this and perhaps the highest point in Kent. The group of beeches rise from land 800 feet above sea level, but there is no ancient church here and the oldest building is the Elizabethan Ivy Cottage. The Cock Inn, Rosemary Cottage, Cypress Cottage and Ide Cottage are all eighteenth century. But there are commanding views overlooking the reservoir which was built in 1969 and several ancient buildings were removed from the area to make way for the project, to be lovingly reconstructed at the Weald & Downland Open Air Museum at Singleton in Sussex.

Lullingstone Roman Villa, built around AD125 with steps leading down to a cellar.

Route: From the church go on to the roundabout, turning right past the Cock Inn and down Camberwell Lane, keeping ahead at the footpath signpost to Brook Place. At the lane turn right along a footpath between The Rambles and Cordons Farm, maintaining a straight direction to the lane, where turn right then left over a stile beside a metal gate opposite Brook Place (1721). Take the right fork into the woods, turning left at the cross-tracks and forking right. Leave the wood skirting it on the right, over a stile and along an enclosed path to a track where turn left over a ford and through Manor Farm. Continue up the track to a stile off left as the track continues right. Over stile and across field, crossing two more stiles to the church at Sundridge Place. (3 miles/4.8km)

SUNDRIDGE.
Mentioned in the Domesday Book, the manor was a valuable property long before the Norman Conquest, and was granted to the See of Canterbury by Earl Godwin, father of King Harold. The church of St Mary the Virgin dates from the thirteenth century and possesses three fifteenth century brasses; one of 1429 showing Roger Isley in rich armour and with a lion at his feet; a civilian of 1460 in a fine example of the costume of his time; and Thomas Isley with his wife and their thirteen children. A stone in the chancel in memory of a rector is older still, for he was preaching here in 1310, long before the church had aisles. Tall fifteenth century windows fill the church with light and in the chancel walls are set the fragments of ancient sculpture, one an angel with a shield. Two other busts face each other in the chancel, sculptured by Anne Seymour Damer, who lies in the memorial chapel.

Route: From the lych gate take the path left through the churchyard, through the kissing gate and along an enclosed path. DO NOT cross the stile ahead but turn right parallel with the A25, emerging at a track where turn right by Warren Farm Stables. Over a stile as the track ends, continuing through a nursery to the road which cross straight over, then through the car park, keeping ahead at the waymarker across the next field then left along the edge of the field following. Turn right for 75 yards (69m) before turning left through a metal clapper stile and across the roads, turning right over the bridge across the A21 then left over the slip road and down the steps to a bridge. Cross a stile then bear left across the field to a metal kissing gate to the left of the Residential Home. Left at the road and left again at the junction signposted Chevening into Chipstead. Immediately beyond the Bricklayers Arms turn right at the public footpath signpost to the lake where turn left onto the Darent Valley Path, which follow round the lake before turning off left across the field immediately beyond the sluice. Straight across at cross-tracks and under the M26, turning off right in a few steps and up a bank to the road. Right here then left at the Rose and Crown, signposted Otford, turning right at the North Downs Way immediately before Donnington Manor Hotel and follow the waymarkers over the railway and down the lane to the T-junction. Turn right here towards Otford, turning left alongside the River Darent following the Darent Valley Path to the road, where turn left into Shoreham. (6 miles/9.6km)

SHOREHAM. Situated in the Darent valley, this ancient village is overlooked by the large white cross carved into the hillside by the villagers to commemorate their dead in two World Wars. Samuel Palmer came here from London in 1826 and lived at Water House, the white painted house near the bridge, where he spent seven years and painted some of his most visionary work. William Blake visited Palmer and John Wesley came here once a year for forty years to visit his friend Vincent Perronet, who preached at the church for almost two generations.

The church of St Peter and St Paul dates back to Norman times and has a fine timbered porch, a rood screen that extends the full width of the church and has 42 compartments in eight bays. The organ case dates back to 1730 and came from Westminster Abbey where it encased the choir-organ given by George II for his Coronation. The pulpit also came form Westminster Abbey and the Borrett family has a small gallery of sculptured busts.

Route: Turn right past the war memorial and past Water House to continue along the riverbank to the footbridge, which cross, and after a few paces turn right to rejoin the riverbank. The path then swings away from the river to cross a large field. Continue over a farm road to a path opposite and follow this with a hop field on the right to join the road. Continue ahead along the road past Castle Farm to Kingfisher Bridge and Lullingstone Park Visitor Centre. (Refreshments/Toilets). Follow the path beside the river, continuing past the lake to the Gatehouse at Lullingstone Castle. (2miles/3.2km)

LULLINGSTONE CASTLE. The magnificent Henry VIII gatehouse was built in 1497 of massive proportions and is believed to be one of the earliest brick gatehouses in England. Beyond was once a moat and a further gatehouse which gave entrance to the manor house, now the core of the present house, and this accounts for why there seems such a wide gap between the gatehouse and house. Three-storeyed, the plan of the gatehouse is a rectangle with polygonal turrets attached to the outer face, and polygonal projections from the inner. The level area to the west of the gatehouse is the site of the jousting ground. Sir John Peche, who built the original manor house, took a leading part in the Royal Jousts and his plumed helmet can be seen on view in the State Drawing Room. Most of the present building dates from 1738, though there was a manor house mentioned here in the Domesday Book.

The interior retains its medieval and Tudor layout, the two-storeyed centre of the west front wholly occupied by the hall. In the north-east corner a rusticated arch leads to the staircase and the State Drawing Room occupies the site of the solar in the upper two storeys in the west front north of the hall. It lies end-on to the façade and has a late sixteenth century barrel vault with roundels of Roman Emperors over the fireplace.

Lullingstone Castle. Most of the manor house dates from 1738, though the interior retained its medieval and Tudor layout.

Privately owned. Open April-September. Gardens 12-5; House Fri. & Sat. 2-5; Sundays House and Garden 2-6. Admission charge.

Lullingstone Park. This was used as a decoy airfield for Biggin Hill during World War II and is open to the public. On a hill overlooking the castle a series of Iron Age storage pits have been discovered containing Iron Age and wheel-turned Belgic wares, indicating that there might have been a hillfort there, but if so intensive cultivation has obliterated any traces of it.

St Botolph's church. This little flint building consisting of nave and lower chancel dates back to the fourteenth century, its white walls rising from the green lawns. The figure of Sir John Peche lies under the three arches of the tomb in the chancel and there is a monument to Sir Percival Hart, who inherited from Sir John Peche, and whose family kept the estate for several centuries. Near him lie Sir George Hart and his wife, hand-in-hand since 1587, on a very striking sculptured tomb. The screen is over 500 years old, the pulpit belongs to Queen Anne's day and is it the font kept in a cupboard? of about the same age. The white plaster roof has some charming decoration and each window contains some old glass. The brasses are all in the chancel: Sir William Peche, 1487; Alice Baldwyn, a gentlewoman at the court; Elizabeth Hart, mother of Sir Percival, 1544; and Ann Hall.

St. Botolph's Church, Lullingstone Castle, dates back to the 14th century.

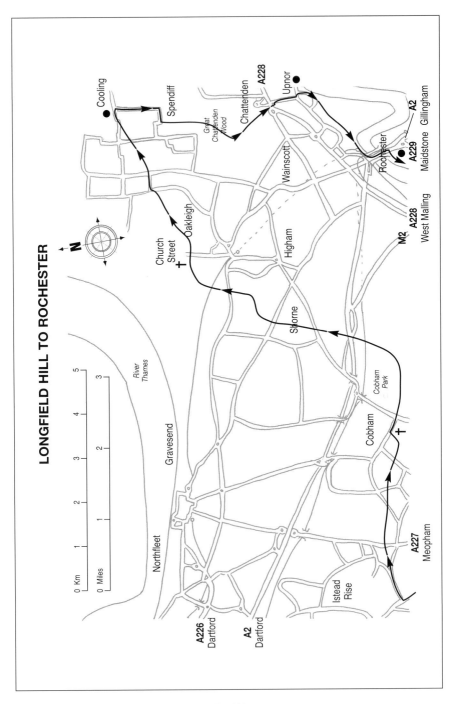

LONGFIELD HILL TO ROCHESTER

Cooling
Spendiff
Great Chattenden Wood
Chattenden
A228
Upnor
A2 Gillingham
A229 Maidstone
Rochester
A228 West Malling
M2
Wainscott
Higham
Church Street
Oakleigh
Shorne
Cobham Park
Cobham
A227 Meopham
Istead Rise
A226 Dartford
A2 Dartford
Northfleet
Gravesend
River Thames

N

| 0 Km | 1 | 2 | 3 | 4 | 5 |
| 0 Miles | 1 | 2 | 3 |

Lullingstone to Cooling Castle

This is the second longest section, and after passing the Roman Villa and Eynsford, there then follows about ten miles across country, skirting the urbanisations of New Ash Green, Hartley and Longfield Hill without getting involved in much of any of them. The route then passes through several orchards before emerging into the churchyard of Cobham, a delightful place with its old college and the legendary Leather Bottle Inn. A path through Cobham Park takes us over the A2 from where a meandering route leads to the impressive ruins of Cooling Castle by the marshes of the River Thames.

Route: Continue to the narrow road, which follow 0.5 mile (0.8km) to the Roman Villa.

LULLINGSTONE ROMAN VILLA. First excavated in 1949, it soon became apparent that here was one of the finest Roman sites in Britain. Excavations continued a further twelve years. A villa was first built here around AD80-90, a very simple affair consisting of a range of rooms linked by a front veranda and a back corridor. At the northern end lay a cellar reached by a flight of wooden steps. The first stone house was built around AD125 and was enlarged between AD150-180 with the addition of a suite of heated baths and a 'cult room', which would have been used in the worship of Roman gods.

It would appear after AD200 the villa was not kept in good repair and part of it was modified to serve as a tannery. By the end of the third century, however, a series of repairs and modifications were undertaken and further alterations took place during the fourth century. In the main part of the villa a large apsidal dining room was built adorned with a fine mosaic depicting Europa abducted by Jupiter in the guise of a white bull. This is still in excellent condition. The dining room opened into a large reception area and on the floor another mosaic incorporating a picture of Bellerophon astride Pegasus slaying the Chimaera. About this time a Christian chapel was built over the old cellar and is the only example of a chapel to be found inside a Roman home in Britain, making it one of the oldest places of Christian worship discovered in the country. It was adorned with painted wall plaster showing Christians with arms outstretched in a position of prayer. The villa was eventually destroyed by fire in the fifth century.

Close by were three other buildings: a simple circular temple of the second century, a temple mausoleum built in the fourth century in Romano-Celtic style with a central cella surrounded by an ambulatory, and a large granary of the late third century. Remains of the lost church of St John the Baptist, Lullingstone, probably Saxo-Norman, have also been found, sited over the temple mausoleum.

Tour of Lullingstone Villa: To the left of the entrance is the Deep Room which was probably used for storing grain, but in the late second century a pit containing ritual water was sunk into the centre of the room and a niche built in the left hand wall. This was decorated with a painting of three water-nymphs, the head of one is still in good condition, with green leaves in her hair and water tumbling from her breasts.

In the fourth century the room on the first floor above the Deep Room was converted into a Christian house-chapel. Proof of this was discovered from painstaking reconstruction of painted plaster found in tiny fragments among fallen debris in the Deep Room. The original wall plaster is now in the British Museum, although a modern painting showing part of it is displayed opposite. Next pass the reconstruction drawing displayed in what had been the front corridor of the house.

Now comes the bath-suite which was built towards the end of the second century. The various rooms, hot, tepid and cold were labelled and there are two cold water pools at one end, the larger being a third century addition. The hot room had a pool for hot water in the apse on the left. The fixtures of the baths are not well preserved, only a few pilae (supporting pillars) remain, having been mainly demolished in the fourth century.

Turning the corner is the well which supplied the house with water, and from here, away to the right, is the larger cold plunge-bath in its entirety.

Passing the reconstructed portion of roofing, go up to the balcony and look down on the whole building. In one room the large fourth century pot marks the site of a possible kitchen. The part nearest is the dining room for the master and his guests. The semi-circular apse is rare in Britain and the mosaic has been partly disfigured during the final conflagration.

The mosaic in the principal room depicts Bellerophon astride Pegasus killing the Chimaera. Heads of the Seasons fill the four corners, although Autumn was destroyed when a fence was being erected in the eighteenth century. On leaving the villa turn left and follow the path up the slope. A small circular temple erected around AD80-90 has been marked out in modern materials, but the site of the adjacent mausoleum has now been backfilled.

English Heritage. Opening Times: 1st April-30th September 10-6 daily; 1st October-30th November 10-4 daily; 1st December-31st January 10-4 (Wed &

Sun); 1st February-31st March 10-4 daily. Closed 24th-26th December and 1st January. Admission charge.

Route: Continue along road, with river on right, for 0.75 mile (1.2km) passing under the railway viaduct into Eynsford.

EYNSFORD. A picturesque village with medieval buildings huddled around a small hump-backed stone bridge over the Darent. The sixteenth century half-timbered Plough Inn and neighbouring jettied houses on the west bank of the river are noteworthy.

Church of St Martins began as a tripartite Norman building, but has since been largely restored with a fine spire and intricately decorated west door. It has an attractive chancel raised on three steps, its east window set in a thirteenth century apse, a vaulted roof of blue, a piscina 700 years old with a rare double basin, two of its windows are Norman and its arch is a beautiful piece of fourteenth century craftsmanship. The 500-year-old font is carved with roses and the porch contains two stone coffins. The sanctuary has a fine piece of carved stone in its walls and the tomb in the Bosville chapel is hidden by the organ.

Route: Turn right out of the churchyard along the A225 towards Farningham. The entrance to the Castle is clearly marked between houses opposite the Castle Inn.

The Castle was built by William de Eynsford in the first years of the twelfth century. He was a humble knight who held the manor as a tenant of the Archbishop of Canterbury, and he raised a low mound beside the river Darent and built a wooden tower on top. Soon afterwards he built a flint curtain wall

Eynsford Castle, built by William de Eynsford early 12th century. Most of its curtain wall still remains.

Eynsford Castle. A gate tower once occupied this entrance but has been reduced to its foundations.

520 feet round, most of which still remain, some still 30 feet high in places. A gate tower was added, now reduced to its foundations, in order to strengthen the entrance, and about the same time a stone hall replaced the original wooden tower. This was intended as purely residential and cannot be described as a keep; indeed the absence of a keep is quite unusual for such a construction belonging to the twelfth century. William de Eynsford quarrelled with Thomas Becket and after the latter's murder he was filled with remorse and vowed never to live in the castle again. When the de Eynsford family died out in 1261 the castle remained deserted and was later ransacked during a dispute over ownership. It was later abandoned, though a Tudor house occupies the outer bailey.

English Heritage. Freely accessible all year 10-6 (10-4 in winter). May be closed Monday and Tuesday in December and January. Closed 24th-26th December and 1st January

Route: Turn left back onto the A225 and right into Priory Lane, continuing along the byway to Beesfield Farm. Turn right at the road and left at Donkey Lane to the A20, crossing straight over and heading diagonally right across the field, keeping ahead at the cross-tracks to the road beside a small copse. Immediately turn left at the public footpath signpost, following the path left to the M20, turning left alongside it before crossing over it by the footbridge and keeping ahead to Horton Wood. Turn right into the wood, keeping alongside it on the left, under the power lines and ahead across two paddocks to the road. Turn left alongside the hedge to a stile leading onto the crossroads, where turn off right down Speedgate Hill to the T-junction, continuing ahead at the public footpath signpost. Turn off left at the public footpath towards the wood, which enter and leave en route to Fawkham Manor, a fair sized Victorian mansion with half-hipped gables and diagonal oriel. It was built of flint and brick in 1866-9 by an elderly E.B. Lamb for his own use. Cross straight over the road, bearing left onto the metalled track across the golf course, keeping right of the club house and following the path to the 15th tee. Just beyond the seat turn left to pass under the power lines in the copse, then bear right to the road. At the road turn left and then right just before the Black Lion public house, forking left as the way ahead leads to the spire of Hartley church. At the main road turn left past the telephone kiosk, bearing right at Manor Lane, following it round right and then immediately left at the public footpath, following the path alongside Greygate and a small copse on the left. DO NOT enter Hartley Wood, instead skirt right alongside it, cutting across the tip of the wood to the road. Straight across here, keeping right alongside the railway before turning left over the bridge across it to the B260 at Longfield Hill. Left here and in a few paces right, following the road past Nurstead Hill Farm. Ignore the road off left and as it bends right, keep ahead at the public footpath, under the power lines and straight across the A227 into a small wood. On leaving the wood the Wealdway soon comes in from the left, continuing ahead above Nurstead Court, one of the most famous small medieval houses in the county. The Wealdway continues along the bridleway, but turn off left onto the public footpath into the wood, continuing straight across at the road and at the cross-tracks to the next road. Right here then left and as the footpath swings round right, cross straight over at the cross-tracks by the edge of a copse. Continue ahead through the orchard, crossing straight over the road and bearing left before turning right to pass under two sets of power lines to join another track through the orchard. Keep ahead now turning left at the lane and through the churchyard to Cobham. (10 miles/16 km)

COBHAM.
The Romans were here and built a fine villa which was abandoned shortly before the Anglo-Saxons settled here. In 1362 Sir John de Cobham founded a college consisting of a master and four priests, increased to eleven by 1389, to say masses for the souls of his ancestors. Under the will of the 10th Lord Cobham the college buildings were adapted as twenty almshouses in 1598, and as such they remain to this day. The fourteenth century college was built round two quadrangles close to the south side of the church. The south court of the college is almost totally ruined now.

College open April-September daily 10-7; October-March daily 10-4

Church of St Mary Magdalene is mid-thirteenth century and built of downland flint with a Kentish ragstone tower. In its chancel is the largest collection of memorial brasses in the world - eighteen in all and covering a period of 200 years. The oldest is Lady Joan Cobham dated 1320 and the majority of them portray the de Cobhams and the Brookes, lords of the manor of Cobham. Behind the altar rail lies Sir George Brooke, 9th Lord Cobham, in an alabaster chest erected in 1558. Set above the sloping churchyard at its western end Stone House was originally the college school-house.

Opposite the church is the Leather Bottle Inn, which started life as a modest cottage. It was a favourite hostelry of Charles Dickens, which he immortalised in *Pickwick Papers*.

Cobham Park lies at the eastern end of the main street and houses Cobham Hall which was built in the sixteenth century of red brick and Caen stone. It was the residence of the Earls of Darnley and stands in the middle of a vast wooded deer park. Its four domed towers, clusters of Tudor chimneys, wonderful porches and fascinating windows has a room which was furnished to receive Elizabeth I - but she never came. Today it is a girl's school and is open to the public during part of the Easter holidays and during August.

Route: Continue along the byway into Cobham Park, bearing left at Lodge Farm. Opposite Cobham Hall, take the footpath off left, through the metal kissing gate, taking the left fork across the golf course and into the wood. At the road turn left under the railway, then cross the bridge over the A2, turning off right to Park Pale.

Leather Bottle Inn, Cobham, made famous by Charles Dickens which he immortalised in 'Pickwick Papers'.

Cooling Castle, built after French raiders caused devastation on the Hoo Peninsular in 1379.

Follow the path round left to meet the road at Shorne Ridgeway, continuing ahead to the T-junction, crossing the road to continue ahead along a footpath skirting the wood on the right and crossing another footpath before reaching the A226. Cross the road to continue along the back of the buildings before turning off right to a track, where turn left to the house on the road as another track comes in from the left. Cross straight over and past King's Farm, and where the track peters out continue ahead, keeping to the left alongside a ditch. Near the end of the field cross the stile on the left, crossing the railway tracks before following an enclosed path round the railway works to the road. Left here under the bridge and right at the public footpath signpost immediately beyond it. Follow an obvious route to the road at Church Street, where cross straight over and continue to Oakleigh Lodge, where turn left at the cross-tracks at the end of the fence, crossing the stream and keeping ahead to cross it again before crossing the next field diagonally right under two power lines. Left at the road, turning right just past Buckland Farm then left onto the B2000. Right at the next public footpath at Oast Cottage and right again onto the bridleway at the T-junction. In a few steps turn left at the footpath to the road, turning right beside Gattons Farm and turning off left at the waymarkers across the fields, keeping to the left of the hedge to the road. Follow the road round right to Cooling Castle. (9.75 miles/15.7km)

COOLING CASTLE. In 1379 French raiders caused devastation on the Hoo peninsula, so Cooling was built for Sir John de Cobham with coastal defence in mind. The sea has since receded, leaving only marshland in its wake.

Cooling Castle. The well-preserved outer gatehouse built by Thomas Crump, a local mason.

The outer gatehouse is the work of Thomas Crump, a local mason, but the castle saw no action against foreign invaders, but did become embroiled in civil strife. In 1554 Sir Thomas Wyatt sought the aid of Lord Cobham in the rebellion which he was organising to prevent Queen Mary marrying Philip of Spain. Lord Cobham wisely refused to get involved whereupon Wyatt marched to Cooling and breached the castle walls by cannon fire in the space of a few hours. After that the castle was abandoned and allowed to fall into ruin.

It would have appeared more formidable when the moat was full of water. The outer curtain wall and its rounded angle towers are now in a ruinous state, but the outer gatehouse is well preserved. The inner courtyard is reached through another gate-house flanked by rounded turrets. Keyhole gun ports appear here and elsewhere in the walls. To the right of the gatehouse the curtain is embellished with alternate panels of stone and flint, creating a chequered effect. The corner tower here has vanished but the round towers at the other three corners, along with much of the intervening curtain, still stand.

Privately owned and not open to the public.

WALKING TOUR OF ROCHESTER

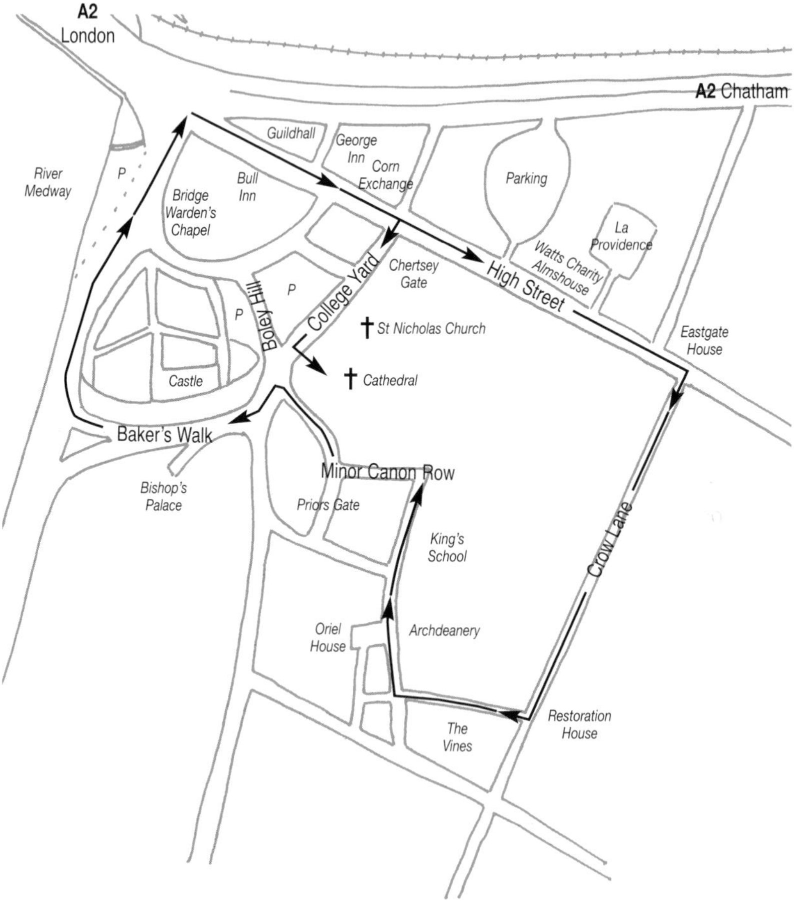

A2
London

A2 Chatham

River
Medway

P

Guildhall

George
Inn

Corn
Exchange

Bull
Inn

Bridge
Warden's
Chapel

Parking

La
Providence

Watts Charity
Almshouse

Chertsey
Gate

High Street

College Yard

Boley Hill

P

P

† St Nicholas Church

Eastgate
House

Castle

† Cathedral

Baker's Walk

Bishop's
Palace

Minor Canon Row

Priors Gate

King's
School

Crow Lane

Oriel
House

Archdeanery

The
Vines

Restoration
House

Cooling to Rochester

A relatively short section this, fairly wooded and quite dramatic. Much of the land is MOD property so imperative to keep to the footpaths, but it soon leads on to the A228, across which is the approach road into Upnor. From here we rejoin the Saxon Shore Way and follow its route above the old lime and cement works, which have now been transformed into an enormous industrial area and thankfully cause us no inconvenience whatsoever. The approach into Rochester is majestic and dramatic and is one of the highlights of the entire walk!

Route: Continue past the castle, turning right at the road junction and following the road under the railway. Keep to the road as it bends right by New Barn, staying ahead at Spendiff as the road bends right again, and turning left onto the footpath immediately after the last house. Keep ahead through Great Chattenden Wood, keeping ahead at the track, and turning right at the crossroads by the MOD buildings, following the path into the wood. Turn left at the footpath sign in the wood, crossing the clearing and entering the wood again. Emerging onto open ground, skirt the small wood on the right before heading diagonally left to the road at The Mount. Left at the road, turning off left at the public footpath signpost by the pond. Take the footpath opposite, beside the stream, turning left over stile and bridge to continue on the opposite side of the stream to the A228, where turn left then right at the public footpath signpost to the road. Right here, following the footpath alongside the road to the crossroads, where keep ahead along the road to Upnor Castle. (5 miles/8km)

UPNOR CASTLE. Sir Richard Lee interrupted his work on the fortifications at Berwick-on-Tweed to design this fort, which was to guard the approach to the new dockyards at Chatham, across the river Medway. Work began in 1559, but construction dragged on for eight years and it took another century before it was to face enemy action. Sir Richard abandoned the familiar geometrical shape of Henry VIII's castles, for its defences needed only to be directed eastward, facing upriver towards the estuary. So it was built comprising of an oblong blockhouse set in the middle of a screen wall terminating at each end in a stair turret. It had a triangular bastion in front of the main building with gun platforms and stockade, and in 1599 the landward defences were improved by Arthur Gregory, by linking the side turrets with the main block and continuing the walls back to enclose a rectangular courtyard. In the centre of the west wall a gatehouse was built, with rectangular corner

Rochester Castle. The west front, facing the castle, is one of the finest examples of 12th century ornamental Norman architecture in England.

towers on the inner side, and a drawbridge. However, since only one side of the bastion faced upriver, it was to discover to its cost that there were insufficient gun emplacements to fire effectively on an approaching fleet.

In 1667 the castle's ineffectiveness against the very test it was built to withstand was put to the test when the Dutch fleet under Admiral de Ruyter sailed up the Medway and set fire to the English fleet. It failed the test miserably and two years later Sir Bernard de Gomme's blockhouses on both sides of the river reinforced the defences. But they never saw action again. Upnor was relegated to the role of storehouse and magazine and military occupation of one kind or another continued until the Second World War.

A Dickensian street of weatherboarded and stock-brick cottages runs down the hill to the water's edge south of the castle enclosure, from where there are good views across the river to the docks at Chatham.

English Heritage. Opening Times: 1st April-30th September, daily 10-6 1st-31st October, daily 10-4. Admission charge.

Route: Follow the footpath from the castle, following the Saxon Shore Way and Cycle Route 1 signs to the Medway Bridge which cross into Rochester. (3 miles/4.8km)

ROCHESTER. This ancient city on the lower reaches of the river Medway is a major port and an industrial and commercial centre and part of the Medway towns complex, which also includes Strood, Chatham and Gillingham. There has been a settlement here since before Roman times; its Celtic name Durobruae means 'the bridge of the stronghold'. Indeed the crossing over the Medway at this point on the route from London to Canterbury and Dover gave the site its early strategic importance. Appreciating its value the Romans built a walled city here around 43AD and traces of their defences are still evident in the Esplanade and Eagle Alley, where they were later incorporated into Saxon and medieval fortifications.

Charles Dickens has close associations with the city, having spent his early childhood here between 1817-1821. His father worked in the Navy Pay Office at Chatham and he used Rochester more often than any other place bar London in his books. Many of the buildings still standing from his day are frequently referred to in *Great Expectations*, *Pickwick Papers* and *Uncommercial Traveller*. His last, unfinished novel, *The Mystery of Edwin Drood*, is based entirely in Rochester, which he called Cloisterham.

Sir Francis Drake, Admiral Lord Nelson, Sir John Hawkins and Samuel Pepys are all associated with the city, thanks to their naval connections, for the Medway was once the prime naval port of their day. But it is the castle that dominates this wonderful place, and little wonder, for at 125 feet to the top of the corner turrets it is the tallest of the tower keeps of England.

Rochester Castle. The Romans had a camp here and later the Saxons built *Hrofe Caestre*, a fortified enclosure of seven acres and a motte known as Boley Hill. The manor was bestowed on Odo, Bishop of Bayeux, by William the Conqueror, who later decreed that a castle should be built here. Bishop Gundulph undertook the task in about 1080, but it was William de Corbeuil, then Archbishop of Canterbury, who built the keep after being granted custody of the castle and the office of constable in 1126.

The keep is little altered from the original, built of ragstone rubble with dressings of Caen stone and is over 100 feet high with walls 12 feet thick. It was the first great square keep to be constructed in an English castle and it was soon put to the test. The archbishops of Canterbury acted as constables until 1215, when Stephen Langton handed the castle over to the Magna Carta rebels. Then followed one of the most gripping of medieval sieges, with King John assembling a large force in an attempt to regain this important stronghold.

William d'Albini held the castle against King John for three months, sustaining prolonged catapult bombardment which failed to breach the walls. In an act of desperation the king's forces drove a mine beneath the south angle of the curtain wall and caused it to collapse. The garrison fell back into the keep and another mine brought the adjacent corner of the keep crashing down, but even this did not compel the defenders to surrender. They retreated behind the cross-wall and continued to hold out, but finally a lack of provisions forced them to surrender. The astute visitor will notice that when the south-east turret was rebuilt it was made round, while the remaining three are angular. Why remains a mystery to this day.

In 1216 the French Dauphin Louis recaptured Rochester for the barons and in the 1220s Henry III repaired the damaged stronghold, only for it to have to endure another battering in 1264, this time at the hands of Simon de Montfort. The curtain was breached once again but the keep was saved by the fortuitous arrival of a royal relieving force. The damage sustained on this attack was left untouched until the latter years of Edward III, who refortified the castle in response to the growing threat of French raids.

In 1381 it was captured by Wat Tyler's rebels, with the support of the local townsfolk and after this it fell into decay, although Edward IV spent some time and money trying to repair it. Its constable from 1413 onwards was Lord Cobham, whose family were involved in Wyatt's Rebellion of 1554 (see page 90).

Walker Weldon, whose family received the estate from James I, began to dismantle the keep, selling its timbers to the builders of the brewhouse and its stone to a firm of masons. In 1738 all that remained was offered to a local paviour. The estate then passed to the family of the Earls of Jersey from whom Rochester Corporation took a lease in 1870, buying the freehold fourteen years later. Today it is in the hands of English Heritage as an ancient monument.

Tour of the Castle: The height of the keep is accentuated by its relatively small floor area, compared, say, to that of Dover. It is five stages high, including the 'double' storey containing the hall and solar and its unique feature is the Caen stone wellshaft running through the centre of the keep, which served each of the floors.

Originally the only entrance was at first floor level, via a forebuilding. This has a tunnel-vaulted basement, which most probably was originally a dungeon beneath the entrance vestibule, and is a tall and narrow projection, higher than most forebuildings, though it does not rise the full height of the keep. Above is the chapel, an austere affair, reached from the body of the keep. A doorway at the head of the steps leads into the first floor while a second, at right angles, leads into the keep proper, with a portcullis slot. A cross-wall divides the keep into two equal halves and a tunnel-vaulted wall passage opens onto the upper level of the hall as a gallery. The windows here are unusually large for a

Rochester Castle from the Medway Bridge. The keep was built by William de Cordeuil in 1126.

Norman keep, presumably because of the height they were considered to be out of reach of siege towers. The floor above the gallery is also well lit, indeed a luxury of its day.

The Hall occupies the third and fourth storeys, and here the cross-wall becomes an arcade of two plus two bays on massive round piers with square capitals. A screen ran along the lower part of the arcade, represented today by an enriched doorway in the west bay. The main doorway into the Hall was on the north side and there are fireplaces north and south, with flues running obliquely through the wall.

The curtain wall still runs around most of the bailey, which today has been laid out as a park. The wall varies in height and is clearly of various dates. Towards the river, where the curtain follows the line of the old Roman city wall, the ragstone is laid in herringbone courses, characteristic of Gundulf's time. The southern section with the circular bastion is quite clearly post-assault while on the eastern side the larger blocks of stone belong to a fourteenth century wall-strengthening project. Facing the cathedral used to be the old gatehouse, but the present entrance can be found at the north corner of the bailey, through a neo-Norman gateway of 1872, piercing a bastion built to command the once fortified bridge across the Medway.

English Heritage. Opening Times: 1st April-30th September, daily 10-6 1st October-31st March, daily 10-4. Closed Christmas Day, Boxing Day and New Years Day. Admission charge.

Walking Tour of Rochester: From the castle descend the steps to the Esplanade, where turn right for the Bridge Warden's Chamber and Chapel. A plaque on the wall depicts the site where the medieval stone bridge built by Sir Robert de Knolles and Sir John de Cobham in around 1387, and demolished in 1856, crossed the river opposite this spot. It is now the boardroom of the Bridge Wardens, a trust formed in 1391 to administer the vital crossing over the Medway, on whose authority the second, adjacent road bridge was built in 1970. Adjoining is the ancient Bridge Chapel which is, alas, inaccessible. Turn right into the High Street with its Georgian frontages and even older backs. To enhance its atmosphere traditional lamp columns have been introduced, the footpaths have been widened, making it semi-pedestrianized, and a red brick carriageway has replaced the tarmacadam road surface. Along its length are a variety of attractive shops, antique and craft centres, tea rooms, coffee shops and olde worlde pubs, providing the visitor with a pleasant, leisurely saunter back through time. Behind a mundane shop front at No. 4 is Draper's Museum of Bygones, covering three floors and setting out sixteen old shops including a chemist, toyshop, sweetshop and haberdashery.

The Bull Hotel, or to give it its proper title the Royal Victoria and Bull Hotel after Queen Victoria slept there in 1836, was formerly an old coaching inn on the original Dover road. Note the impressive coat-of-arms over the main gateway - not Victoria's, but that of George III and Queen Charlotte. First recordings of its existence date back to 1555 and its entrance hall, fine staircase and ballroom are all the original, well preserved. Charles Dickens used it as his 'Blue Boar' in *Great Expectations* and he also wrote how Mr Pickwick attended a ball here in the first floor ballroom.

Almost opposite is the very fine Guildhall, built in 1687 and surmounted by a ship weather vane, added in 1780. The main Hall interior has an outstanding plaster ceiling, the gift of Admiral Sir Cloudsley Shovel, and on its walls hang some interesting portraits. The Guildhall became a museum in 1979 and was refurbished in 1994 to house exhibits on local history from the Stone Age to modern times, including geology, archaeology, maritime and industrial history along with political and social history of the area. A two-tier gallery recreates one of the Medway prison ships from the Napoleonic War, with audiovisual effects leaving little to the imagination.

The George Inn has a fine four-bay undercroft dating back to *c.*1320 and Admiral Sir Cloudsley Shovel's coat-of-arms decorates the clock of the old Corn Exchange, which he had built for the city in 1706. He represented the town in three parliaments under William III and one under Queen Anne as well as serving as a distinguished naval officer. He is buried in the south choir of Westminster Abbey.

Almost opposite is the much named Chertsey Gate at the entrance of College Yard on the corner of Boley Hill. Formerly known as Cemetery Gate and now known as College Gate, Charles Dickens used it to great effect as the home of John Jasper in *The Mystery of Edwin Drood*. It was one of the old gates into the monastery precincts and dates from the early fifteenth century, but had a black clapperboard house slapped on top of it in the eighteenth century. It is not open to the public. Just up from here are two houses of worship. St Nicholas church dates from 1421 and stands within the limits of the ancient city adjoining the Cathedral. Prior to this date the parishioners did not have a place of worship of their own, being given the right of offering their devotion at an altar in the Cathedral. This altar has an interesting history and bears direct result in the actual building of St Nicholas. The monks of the Cathedral claimed all profits of the altar, causing dissatisfaction among the parishioners and a dispute which had to be settled at the court of Rome. After much deliberation it was decreed that the altar be set aside for the celebration of Mass for the parishioners at an hour not to interfere with the monks performing their religious services. This was decided on the 6th April 1312. Over a century later the present church was built to overcome the problem once and for all, consecrated in 1423 by Bishop Chourles of Dromore in the absence of the Bishop of Rochester. From its induction St Nicholas has always been the civic church of the city and underwent a restoration in 1621. Further repairs were carried out in 1863 when the galleries were added.

With a dwindling in the population of the parish it soon became evident that the church could not support itself and in December 1971 became redundant, with its parish uniting to become part of the parish of Rochester and St Nicholas became a Chapel of Ease, owned by the Rochester Diocesan Society who became responsible for its future maintenance.

Adjoining is the beautiful Cathedral, the west front of which, facing the castle, is one of the finest examples of twelfth century ornamental Norman architecture in England. Just inside the west door, marked on the floor, is the outline of the eastern end of a small cathedral built in AD604 by Justus, first Bishop of Rochester, on a plot of ground given by King Ethelbert. Justus accompanied St Augustine from Rome and the Cathedral was dedicated to St Andrew until the Reformation. The Norman nave was begun about 1080 by Bishop Gundulf who, apart from building the castle opposite, was also responsible for the building of the White Tower at the Tower of London. He also established the Benedictine Priory of St Andrew here. The great west window, clerestory and roof were added in the late twelfth century.

The monks began enlarging the Cathedral early in the thirteenth century and the tower was raised and a spire added in 1343. The spire was replaced in 1749 and replaced again by the present one in 1905.

The north transept of the nave was erected about 1235 housing many of the finely carved heads which are a feature of the Cathedral. The presbytery, containing the High Altar, also houses many tombs of medieval Bishops of Rochester. The thirteenth century choir stalls are the oldest surviving in England today. The Cathedra - or Bishop's Throne - from which the word cathedral is derived, is nineteenth century.

The crypt or undercroft is of Norman design and is one of the most spacious in England, containing fragments of medieval wall paintings and notable graffiti. The south nave transept houses memorials to Charles Dickens, who wished to be buried here, and also to General Gordon of Khartoum. The Lady Chapel, the last part of the Cathedral to be completed, was built in 1493 in the Perpendicular style.

Outside, the garden was once the centre of life of the old Benedictine Priory, surrounded by a Norman cloister with fine stone carvings, of which parts still remain. Parts of the wall on the south side of the garden are the original Roman city wall. On the east side stands the ruined façade of the Norman Chapter House. Return to the High Street, turning right to Watts Charity Almshouses. Founded under Richard Watts' will in 1579, for a night's lodging 'for six poor travellers, not being rogues or proctors'. It was rebuilt in 1771 on the old lines and the little galleried Elizabethan bedrooms are now open to public view.

A little further down on the left is La Providence, a hospital for French protestants and their descendants residing in Great Britain, which arose from a bequest made in 1708 by a Huguenot refugee who was Master of the King's Buckhounds at the court of King William and Queen Mary and was granted a royal charter by George I in 1718. For more than 250 years La Providence (as the poor Huguenot refugees called it) provided shelter and care 'for those among us who are in distress', first in the City of London and then in Hackney. Its present home, formerly Theobald Square, was opened in 1959 after restoration into flats housing the elderly of Huguenot descent. Under a new charter granted by Elizabeth II in 1953 the direction of La Providence remains in the hands of a Governor, Deputy Governor and Directors who are honoured to maintain this monument in the piety of their ancestors.

Further on still is Eastgate House on which Dickens based the Nun's House in *Edwin Drood*. The house, built in 1590, has been turned into a Charles Dickens Centre with a pictorial history of his life, along with life-size reconstructions of scenes from his books, and miniature theatre sets to provide an education in social history. In the garden is Dickens' chalet from Gads Hill Place where he wrote his last words, and by the gate is an original section of the old Roman cobbled Watling Street.

Retrace steps and turn left into Crow Lane, then right into the small park, opposite the entrance to which stands Restoration House. Built in 1587 it is said Charles II stayed here on the 28th May 1660 at his restoration. Dickens used this house as the 'Satis' House in *Great Expectations.*

Take the right fork at the cross-tracks in The Vines, so called for this is the area where the monks had their vineyard. The avenue of plane trees was planted about 1880, but the 'Seven Sisters' elm trees referred to by Dickens were at the far end of the park, but have had to be felled for safety reasons.

At the end of the park is the Archdeanery on the right, a charming old house, enlarged in 1661. Opposite is Oriel House (1758). Turn right here past King's School, which was re-founded by Henry VIII in 1542, then left along the delightful eighteenth century Minor Canon Row, mentioned in *Edwin Drood,* and was at one time home of Dame Sybil Thorndike while her father was resident here. It is of interest to note that No. 7 was originally built for the organist, and is still so used today.

Priors Gate to the left at the end of Minor Canon Row is the most perfect of three surviving fourteenth century monastic gates, but continue ahead to Boley Hill, where on the left is the old Bishop's Palace where Erasmus stayed with the saintly Bishop Fisher, who was martyred for his faith by Henry VIII. Keep left of the castle down Bakers Walk back to the Esplanade.

Rochester Castle. The castle was besieged several times but the keep suffered only minor damage.

ROCHESTER TO MAIDSTONE

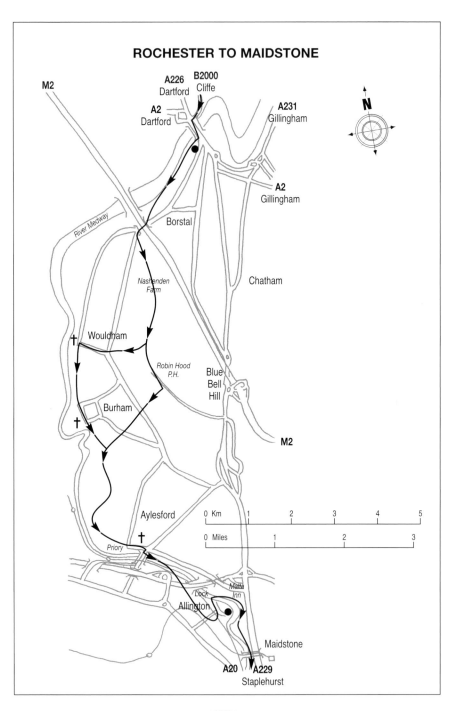

Rochester to Allington

This section sees us back on the North Downs Way before joining the Medway Valley Walk into Aylesford, with its ancient Priory, commanding church and old river crossing. The Medway is Kent's premier river and remains tidal at this point and we follow it as far as Allington Lock, where its might is controlled prior to flowing through the county town of Maidstone. It is possible to re-cross the river at this point and it is along this section where there are good views of Allington Castle, once open to the public but now, sadly, no longer.

Route: Follow the Esplanade towards the M2 bridge across the Medway, continuing ahead at Baty's Marsh as the road swings left. Continue ahead on the Medway Valley Path, past Medway Bridge Marina, turning left at the yellow waymarker up past the garages to the road. Right at the road through Borstal village, under the M2 then immediately left onto the North Downs Way. Turn right at Nashenden Farm House oasts and over railway, and once the Way meets the wider track a decision has to be made. At some stage it is necessary to descend to the Medway valley and this track, going down right, is one option. To continue along the North Downs Way is the better option, but the later descent is longer and steeper and the state of the Way from Nashenden Farm should be a good indicator of what to expect on this descent. That is to say if the Way is muddy or slippery I would recommend the track option; if conditions underfoot are perfect then the choice is down to you.

If taking the track down here it eventually becomes a metalled lane to the road. Cross straight over down School Lane into Wouldham, once a cement works community. The lych gate of the church is a memorial to the dead of two World Wars, and in the churchyard is the tomb of Walter Burke, purser of the Victory at the Battle of Trafalgar and in whose arms Nelson died. Turn left at the T-junction onto the Medway Valley Walk, keeping ahead as the road swings off left and maintaining a straight direction past Burham Court church.

If keeping to the North Downs Way, keep ahead past Burham Hill Farm, where the Way becomes metalled as far as the Robin Hood public house, and here turn off right at the public footpath. Descend into Burham, crossing straight over at the road, and keeping ahead at the footpath at the T-junction to meet the alternative route at the bend in the next road. (5 miles/8km)

BURHAM. Set under the North Downs it is a typical nineteenth century chalk quarrying village, but its past lies a mile away, down by the river, where the old village used to be. The tower of its redundant church is still visible in the distance, where nearby the Romans hollowed out a temple in the sandbank to worship Mithras, their God of the Sun.

Route: Keep ahead where the road peters out, past the gate and along Old Church Road. Follow the main track past the metal gates, turning left at the Medway Valley Walk waymarker where the paths divide by the overhead power lines. Follow the path through the old works to the road, which follow ahead to road at Aylesford Priory. (3 miles/4.8km)

AYLESFORD. It was here where the English established their power, one day in AD449, when English history began, the day that Hengist and Horsa brought their forces and fought and defeated the ancient Britons.

Eight hundred years later Baron Richard de Grey, lord of the manor of Aylesford, joined Richard of Cornwall on a crusade to the Holy Land. There they found a small community of hermits living a life of prayer and silence on Mount Carmel, but they were under constant attack from the Moslems, so they offered to take some of them back to England, promising them safe houses once they were there. Half of them went to Northumberland while the other half followed de Grey back to Aylesford where he granted them a small plot of land on the banks of the river Medway. Here the Carmelites, as they became known, built a small chapel surrounded by a number of cells. The site of this chapel was on the place where the present shrine stands. Baron de Grey was buried in the chapel in 1271 and his descendants continued to support the order, granting them donations that enabled them to erect more substantial buildings.

By the beginning of the fourteenth century the Carmelites had thirty houses in England, although Aylesford remained one of the smallest and by 1538 the community there 'surrendered' the house and set off to seek employment as best they could.

After the Dissolution the property passed into the hands of Sir Thomas Wyatt of nearby Allington Castle, and after his death in 1542 was rented by his son to a John Morse. Unfortunately Wyatt's son lacked his father's diplomatic skills and he became one of the leaders of the abortive Kentish Rising against Queen Mary in 1553 and was executed for his trouble and had all his property taken by the Crown. A few years later Elizabeth I gave the property to Sir John Sedley who turned it into his family residence. He removed the church and one side of the cloisters but added an extra wing to the courtyard, which is now the reception office. He also built the farm which stands near the entrance to The Friars. At his death he left money for the construction of a large almshouse which is now the Hospital of the Holy Trinity in the village.

In 1633 The Friars was bought by Sir Peter Rycaut, son of a Dutch merchant, and in the Civil War he sided with the Crown, which was an unfortunate choice, for the Parliamentarians sequestrated his property and interned him and his wife in Upnor Castle. They used The Friars as a magazine, withstanding two Royalist onslaughts before being seized in 1648.

The Rycaut's sold The Friars to Caleb Banks after the Civil War and his son started to restore it into a country mansion, adding a new wing at the end of the cloisters and reversed the approach to the house so that the main entrance was through the old cloister area. The grounds were landscaped and the enclosed garden with its entrance and orangery at the far end date from this time. Following his death the property passed to his daughter who was married to the son of the Earl of Nottingham, who in 1714 was created Earl of Aylesford.

During the nineteenth century it was rented to various tenants and by 1907 became empty and remained so for several years. Around 1920 it was rented by Mrs Woolsey who cared deeply for the house and spent a lot of time trying to restore it. Unfortunately in 1930 there was a disastrous fire which burnt out the main part of the house, but it did reveal many of the medieval features which had been hidden under later alterations. Mrs Woolsey's daughter and son-in-law, Mr Copley-Hewitt, then bought the property and set about restoring it to as much of its original features as possible, inserting the gothic style windows on the first floor.

During the Second World War it was used by the army after which it again fell into disrepair. In 1949 it was put up for sale and the Carmelites throughout the world contributed in order to purchase back their ancient house. After much restoration work and the construction of the outdoor shrine The Friars was rededicated in 1965 and each year since then has seen large numbers of visitors paying pilgrimage. The village also contains many other interesting old buildings, including The Chequers Inn (1511), The George House (originally built in 1540 and formerly known as The Windmill and George), and The Little Gem (mainly sixteenth century on twelfth century foundations).

The church of Saint Peter and St Paul stands on the hill where the Normans built a church, but all that remains of the original building is the lower portion of the tower, the Roman tiles built into the local stone were plundered from the ruined villa at Eccles. Its site commands a view of the Medway and its ancient bridge built around 1390, replaced an earlier, wooden structure.

The oldest memorials to be found are lying on the ground by the east wall; three coffin covers dating from the thirteenth century. Originally they were inside the church but were removed in 1878 during a restoration. Inside there are two naves, supported by early fifteenth century pillars. The massive octagonal pillars supporting the arches dividing the north and south chancels are fourteenth century and the south chancel arch and roof are not in alignment, giving it a twisted appearance.

On the floor of the north chancel is the oldest brass in the church, to John Cossington and his wife, situated between the communion table and the Colepepper monument and dated 1426. The Colepepper tomb is said to be one of the finest in Kent. On it lie full length figures of Sir Thomas Colepepper and his lady and at the sides the three sons and daughters that succeeded him. Above them hang helmets and gauntlets and crossed swords.

Route: Cross the old bridge now closed to traffic, turning left at the main road. Cross the road to proceed down to the riverbank immediately before the road bridge and continue along the riverbank as far as the level crossing, where cross the railway to continue alongside the track and over the M20. Keep ahead now (ignoring the path left over the railway), turning left at the road and left again where the road divides to Allington Lock. Cross over the lock, turning right past the Malta Inn, following the path to Maidstone. (1.6 miles/2.6km)

ALLINGTON CASTLE.

ALLINGTON CASTLE. The ancient Britons set up a moated village here, the Romans built a villa, the Saxons raised a stronghold on the moated ground and the Normans built a manor house, replacing the Saxon palisading with a wall that still remains. The Norman structure was destroyed by Henry II after the revolt of 1173-4. In 1282 Sir Stephen de Penchester, Constable of Dover Castle and Lord Warden of the Cinque Ports, obtained a licence to crenellate, and it is his building that survives today.

Characteristic of the Edwardian style, it reflects the quadrangular layout but without the least sense of symmetry. Five D-shaped towers of different sizes project from the curtain, though not always at corners, and the gatehouse punctuates near the north-west corner, flanked by half-round turrets (the machicolations above the gateway are modern). Solomon's Tower at the south corner is the largest and may be regarded as an early tower house. Some ruins of a barbican survive on the far side of the moat. The range on the south-west side of the courtyard, known as the Penchester Wing, may incorporate a slightly older manor house, however, once the castle was built the main apartments stood opposite, centred on a hall which still exists though mainly in reconstruction. Only its fifteenth century porch is authentic.

Now comes its time in history, when Sir Henry Wyatt, friend of Henry VII and Henry VIII, bought the castle in 1492, adding the straight two-storeyed range that divides the courtyard into two unequal parts, with a long gallery on the upper floor. The picturesque half-timbered and gabled house tucked into the south-east corner of the curtain wall also dates from the Wyatt period. His son Thomas was a poet and friend of Anne Boleyn but it was his son, also named Thomas, who gave the Wyatt name notoriety. For it was he who led the rebellion against Queen Mary's intended Spanish marriage, forcing his father-in-law at Cooling Castle to join the uprising and got himself executed for his trouble. Following this Allington passed to the Crown and the great hall, chapel and north-east tower were burnt down. For a time John Astley, Master of the Jewels to Elizabeth I lived here, but his descendants moved to Maidstone and the castle was rented to a catholic family named Best. The Astleys sold it to the Marshams and it fell into decay, so when Sir Martin Conway found it in 1905 it was a ruin. He spent the next thirty years restoring it; all the battlements are his work and he rebuilt the hall the way it was. Today only the rear curtain is still in ruins. In 1951 Allington was bought by the Carmelites, which is a quirk of fate, for it was the Wyatts who bought Aylesford at the Dissolution. It is now privately owned and no longer open to the public.

Allington Castle viewed from the river towpath en route to Maidstone.

MAIDSTONE TO HARRIETSHAM

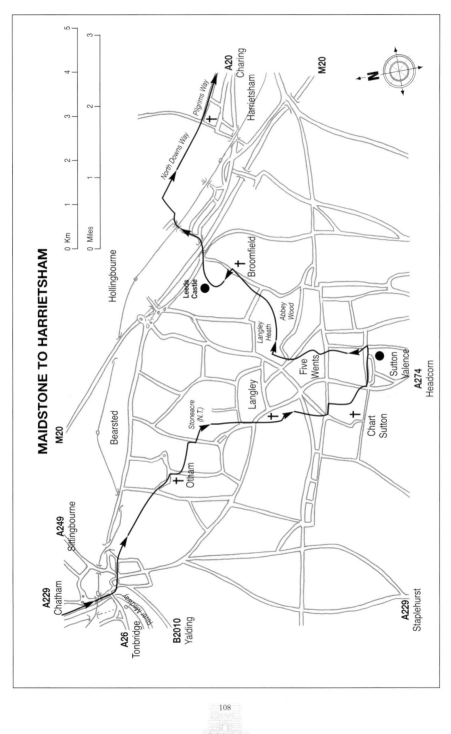

Allington to Leeds Castle

It is surprising how easy it is to negotiate the sprawl of Maidstone, first beside its river and then through its mighty park. The delightful National Trust property Stoneacre is passed en route to the Greensand Way, which leads into the equally delightful Sutton Valence, built on different levels into the hillside, and home to one of Kent's least known castles. From here it is but a short walk to one of the most famous of all castles, Leeds, beautifully set amid rolling parkland and perched majestically upon its watery mantle, on an island in the middle of a huge lake.

Route: Follow the towpath into Maidstone, passing under both road bridges before turning off left through the arch into Palace Gardens. (2.75 miles/4.4km)

MAIDSTONE. The county town of Kent and once owned by the Archbishops of Canterbury during the Middle Ages from which period many fine buildings still remain. It is almost an embarrassment that we pass through this fine, interesting place without giving it the time it deserves, but suffice to say that we pass the Archbishop's Palace in the gardens which was built in 1348 and belonged to the Archbishops of Canterbury until the Dissolution. It contains a fine panelled banqueting hall and is open by appointment only, although it is used for weddings as Maidstone's Register Office.

Opposite the exit from the park stand the Archbishop's Stables, now housing the Tyrwhitt-Drake Museum of Carriages, the finest collection of horse-drawn carriages in the country. Open daily May - mid-September 1030-1600. Free admission.

All Saints church, a former collegiate church, was built by Archbishop Courtney on the site of the earlier church of St Mary's in 1395. It is renowned for being the "grandest Perpendicular church in England", although it did lose its spire when it was struck by lightning in 1730.

Route: Leave Palace Gardens past All Saints church and turn left into Knightrider Street. Cross straight over at the traffic lights into Mote Road, following it round right signposted Mote Park. Enter Mote Park, keeping left to the cycle route. Beyond the lake turn right, signposted Downsgate cycle route, past Mote House and taking the left fork where the track splits. Leaving the park cross straight over to continue along Deringwood Drive, turning right at Church Road signposted Otham, which follow round to the church. (2.75 miles/4.4km)

OTHAM. The church of St Nicholas stands a mile away from the heart of the village and has Norman and Early English features and a brass to Thomas Hendley, who died in 1599, and had three wives and four children. The church registers show that during the sixteenth century it was required by law for persons to be buried in woollen material and an affidavit was needed with each entry to prove that the law was obeyed.

Route: Left at the public footpath signpost opposite the church, forking left to the road where turn right and in a few steps left to Stoneacre. Follow the road down over the ford and up to the house. (1 mile/1.6km)

STONEACRE. An idyllic half-timbered fifteenth century yeoman's house which was lovingly restored by Aymer Vallance in 1920 and then given to the National Trust. It has a central hall with kingposts and an oak windowsill that is worn with the elbows of people leaning on it for half a millennium to look out through the windows at the typical cottage garden.

National Trust. Open mid-March - mid-October Saturdays and Bank Holiday Mondays 1100-1800. Admission charge.

Route: Continue ahead to the road where turn left, bearing right at New Road signposted Langley to the A274. Cross straight over taking the path to the left of the

Stoneacre, half-timbered 15th century yeoman's house owned by the National Trust.

nursery building to the lake, where follow path left, over a stile and along the field edge to Langley church. (1 mile/1.6km)

LANGLEY.

LANGLEY. St Mary's church was built in the mid-nineteenth century on old foundations and the school and Master's house just north of it were all built by Butterfield. Rumwood Court, off the A274, was originally built in the early sixteenth century and enlarged in 1599. The western half of the house was added in 1896.

Route: Head south out of the churchyard, turning right then left down to the B2163. Right at the road and left opposite Fir Tree Farm to the crossroads where turn left, turning right onto the footpath heading towards the church tower. Turn off left onto the Greensand Way just before Chart Sutton church and follow the track all the way to the A274 and Sutton Valence. Turn right at the road and left beside the King's Head public house, keeping to the top road as far as the Swan Inn where turn right then left into Rectory Lane to the castle. (2.5 miles/4km)

SUTTON VALENCE.

SUTTON VALENCE. The village hangs on the southern slopes of the ragstone hills, built on different levels, cut out of the slopes of the steep hill. The public school, founded by William Lambe, a London clothworker, in 1578, dominates the northern part of the village, but it was completely rebuilt between 1910-14. A row of six almshouses built by Lambe in 1580 have been turned to school use since there were no more poor to live in them.

Behind the school are the excavations of a Roman cemetery, and below that the scant remains of a Norman castle. The castle was built by one of Henry III's many unpopular half-brothers, William de Valence, who married a Pembroke heiress and later became Earl of Pembroke. During de Montfort's rebellion he supported Henry III at Lewes, and after Evesham was made governor of Goodrich Castle. Three Pembrokes owned Sutton Valence until it passed to the Cliffords. When Mildred Clifford, who had four husbands, died, her first husband Sir Edward Harper inherited it. He sold it to Edward Hales, whose family lived here for many years. In 1956 the site was excavated and pottery dating from 1150 was discovered together with parts of the forebuilding and staircase. It was built originally to watch over the road from Maidstone to Lympne, which ran through the Weald below, carrying traffic to the Channel ports.

All that survives today is a small twelfth century square keep about 22 feet across internally. It was built of local ragstone with walls about eight feet thick, with a tunnel-vaulted passage at first floor level in the south wall. Sockets for floor joists are visible here, the only wall of any significant height, and the

Sutton Valence Castle. All that survives is a small 12th century keep with walls about eight feet thick.

Sutton Valence Castle, built to guard the Maidstone to Lympne road, carrying traffic to the channel ports.

angles of the keep are clasped by pilaster buttresses in typical Norman fashion. There was once a curtain around the bailey and the tower in the east wall, which Harold Sands traced in 1902, is now also gone. The castle has been in ruins since the fifteenth century. The castle and manor were owned by the Valence family and in the thirteenth century they gave their name, which is derived from Valencia in Spain, to the village in order to distinguish it from its neighbours, Chart Sutton and East Sutton.

English Heritage. Free access at any time.

St Mary's church was rebuilt in 1823-8 and its exquisite fourteenth century carved altar stone is now displayed in the Victoria & Albert Museum in London.

Route: From the castle retrace steps back to the Swan Inn, turning right beside it and up a steep staircase before turning right onto the Greensand Way. Turn left by a row of trees, keeping ahead through orchard to the road. Cross straight over, bearing diagonally left across next field which leave by way of a plank bridge and almost immediately turn right into a wood. Turn right at the T-junction then bear left into the wood. Cross straight over at road to continue into wood. At the end of the wood cross stile and turn right to continue alongside the wood. Re-enter the wood, keeping ahead at cross-tracks to maintain a straight direction. At the clearing on the left turn left at yellow waymarker, continuing up left side of field. At the road turn right and left by the corrugated barn at Park Barn Farm, heading diagonally right across the field and keeping right at the end of the field. Bear left off the track and along a footpath down to the road where turn left into Broomfield, turning off right to visit the church. (3.5 miles/5.6km)

BROOMFIELD.
It can hardly call itself a hamlet, just a knot of cottages huddling the road out of the lush Len valley. St Margaret's church dates from the thirteenth century and has served all the great owners of Leeds Castle, in whose park it stands, and through a grating can be seen their coffins, including that of Lord Fairfax, who when living entertained a king and when dying asked to be buried in poverty.

Route: Cross the river Len before turning left into Leeds Castle estate, skirting the lake up to the approach road, where turn right to Leeds Castle. (0.5 mile/0.8km)

LEEDS CASTLE.
The Saxons knew this place as Esledes, but it was in 1090 that William II granted the manor to his cousin Hamo de Crevecoeur and in 1119 when Robert de Crevecoeur began to build the first stone castle here. During the Baron's War of Simon de Montfort, Robert de Crevecoeur changed allegiance and was dispossessed by Henry III who granted the castle

to Sir Roger de Leyburn. His son transferred the castle to Edward I and so it came into royal possession and part of what is seen today dates from that period. Edward II did little improvement to the place but Edward III extended the park and greatly improved the castle. Richard II enjoyed Leeds when he was on the throne, but saw the darker side of its captivation when he was held prisoner there for a time following his deposition. Still more building work was undertaken early in the sixteenth century and when Henry VIII came to the throne he made a home of the castle for his first wife, Catherine of Aragon, spending vast sums of money and transforming Leeds into a magnificent castle. But by 1552 the Crown had no further use for Leeds and it was granted to Sir Anthony St Leger, who had served his sovereign well. Sir Anthony's great-grandson did not fare quite so well, for as a financial backer of Sir Walter Raleigh's ill-fated expedition to found an empire overseas, he was forced to sell the castle to cover the costs. His wife's uncle, Sir Richard Smythe, became the next owner in 1618, and although the Smythes did not own the castle long, they were responsible for the rebuilding of the principal buildings at the north end of the main island.

In 1632 the castle was sold to Sir Thomas Culpeper and when, some years later during the Civil War, it was used as a Parliamentarian arsenal, thanks to his son's political inclinations, the castle escaped "being knocked about a bit". Culpeper's son's second cousin, Thomas, 2nd Lord Culpeper, used the dowry of his wealthy wife, Margaret van Hesse to buy Leeds Castle in 1663, and this is where the American involvement in the castle's history takes root.

The 1st Lord Culpeper had been instrumental in helping the young Prince of Wales escape from England to seek exile in France, in repayment for which he was granted more than five million acres of land in Virginia.

Lord Culpeper leased the castle to the government in the 1660s to house Dutch and French prisoners-of-war. On one occasion they set fire to their accommodation, causing damage that remained unrepaired until 1822.

In 1680 Lord Culpeper was appointed Governor of Virginia and he left Leeds Castle to take up residency in America. His daughter married Thomas, 5th Lord Fairfax in 1690, and on her death in 1719, Leeds Castle passed to the Fairfax family. They undertook a large scale programme of improvements, finally passing the castle on to the Rev Dr Denny Martin in 1793 and in 1800 to General Philip Martin, his brother. On his death in 1821 the general's fortune was left to a distant kinsman Fiennes Wykeham, who added his benefactor's name to his own and so became Wykeham Martin, a name that was to have a very great effect on the appearance of the castle as we see it today.

In 1822 the Smythe house was demolished and the New Castle was built. New drives were constructed and the main entrance was moved to where it is today. But all this came at a cost and Wykeham Martin was forced to auction the contents of the castle to foot the bill. Fortunately the trustees of General Philip Martin's will were able to purchase the Leeds Abbey estate, enabling Charles Wykeham Martin to rebuild his family's fortune.

In 1924 the family were forced to sell Leeds Castle in anticipation of crippling death duties and it was bought by Mrs Wilson Filmer, who later became Lady Baillie. She lived longer at Leeds than any other owner and towards the end of her life established the Leeds Castle Foundation to which the castle and surrounding parkland were bequeathed in 1974.

Tour of the Castle: The entrance to Leeds Castle, over the southern end of the lake, was guarded by an unusually complex barbican with a mill attached, which remains reasonably intact. The barbican had three gateways because three roads converged here; to Maidstone (west), Leeds (south) and Lenham (east). Only the Maidstone road arch has much left, a depressed-pointed arch with a portcullis groove. A second arch at right-angles is similarly fortified. A stone bridge with two arches then leads across the moat to the gatehouse.

The gatehouse is Edwardian but remarkably uncharacteristic of the period, with a low, squat tower, a recess for the drawbridge and a later row of machicolations above the entrance. This was part of Edward I's reinforcement of the main island's defences, when a new wall was built up from the bed of the moat, enclosing the whole island, with five D-shaped turrets, two on the west side and three on the east. The walls were reduced to lawn level in the nineteenth century to allow an unimpeded view across the lake and no longer serve as a deterrent, except for the north-east turret, which is still intact with its steep tiled roof.

The isolated block east of the croquet lawn is Maiden's Tower, one of Henry VIII's additions, although Wykeham-Martin added embellishments, particularly to both doorways, and gave it its name in the nineteenth century following the discovery that Christiana Hyde, a recluse, was allowed to live on this site during Richard II's reign. The crenellations were probably added in the early sixteenth century and Lady Baillie converted it back to domestic use after being used as a brewhouse and workshop. Beyond is the New Castle, the neo-Gothic mansion built by Fiennes Wykeham-Martin in the 1820s, and it is this that occupies the site of lavish medieval apartments. The front staircase is adorned with tapestries and pictures which continue along the landing and the Yellow Drawing Room is dominated by The Punchinello's Kitchen by Giambattista Tiepolo the elder (1696-1770). The Palladian chimneypiece is thought to have been brought to Leeds by 7th Lord Fairfax around 1730. The Thorpe Hall Room is so called because the superb Italian marble chimneypiece and the carved pine panelling both came from Thorpe Hall near Peterborough. The Lumley Horseman, in painted oak, is the earliest known equestrian statue in the history of English sculpture and can be seen from the Thorpe Hall Room. It is so called because it was commissioned for Lumley Castle by the 7th Lord Lumley (1533-1609) although the sculptor's identity remains unknown.

On the walls of the front hall are three medieval great swords dating from the fourteenth century and a German sword from around 1500. The Library, Dining Room and Boardroom are often used for conferences so may not always be open for public view. The Library served as a small dining room until 1926 and Lady Baillie used it as a schoolroom when her daughters were receiving their early education. It was redesigned as the Library in 1938 and houses books from Lady Baillie's collection as well as from the library of her father, Lord Queenborough.

In the Dining Room the William IV mahogany dining table contrasts with the white-painted Louis XIV-style chairs, while the Boardroom was rebuilt in 1822 following the destruction caused by French and Dutch prisoners-of-war held at Leeds Castle in the 1660s. There are eighteen bedrooms in the New Castle complex, and these are available to those attending conferences or functions at Leeds Castle.

The Gloriette is reached from the New Castle via a two-storeyed bridge and is a D-shaped structure built around a tiny courtyard. Its lower part, including the tall plinth which rises straight out of the water, is Edward I's work, although almost all the windows are Tudor, except for a few at the lower level, which would suggest the upper storey is wholly Tudor. Weapons and armour spanning several centuries guide the corridor linking the Gloriette to the New Castle.

The Chapel Corridor contains carved furniture and panelling and at each end hangs the armour of a seventeenth century pikeman. The Queen's Room was redesigned in 1984 in order to recreate the luxurious trappings royal ladies might have enjoyed in the fifteenth century. The Queen's Bathroom, like the bedroom, would have had furnishings which were easily dismantled when the queen was not in residence, so they could be easily moved to her next abode, or stored.

In the Queen's Gallery the ragstone fireplace was installed late in the 1920s. Over the years this room has been used as an assembly room and a kitchen and it houses four marble busts of Henry VIII and his three children, all of whom ascended the throne.

Leeds Castle. Most of what exists today dates from the time of Edward I. It enjoys a magnificent lakeland setting.

Fountain Court was originally a much larger courtyard and is much embellished today. The Italianate marble fountain was supplied locally in the late nineteenth century.

The Banqueting Hall is the largest room in the castle, and although it looks authentic it was completely altered for Lady Baillie. The Enghien tapestry is the earliest known in existence, however, dating from between 1513-1535.

The history of the Chapel can be traced back to Edward I, but there have been several changes of use since and many structural alterations. It does contain a late eighteenth century mahogany chamber organ which was believed to have belonged to the Rt Hon Spencer Perceval (1762-1812), the only British Prime Minister to have been assassinated.

The spiral staircase was built by Armand Albert Rateau in 1929 in sixteenth century style during his alterations to the castle, its centrepiece being the carved oak statue of The Laughing Crusader. Off the corridor is the Boardroom, which is open to public view whenever it is not in use for conferences.

Lady Baillie's personal rooms were also created by Rateau and consist of a dressing room, with adjoining bathroom, bedroom and boudoir, now called the Catherine of Aragon Bedroom. The Gloriette is left via a corridor with windows on either side concluding the tour.

Leeds Castle Foundation. Open every day of the year (with one or two exceptions). Grounds open 1000 daily. Castle open April-September 1030-1900; October-March 1030-1700. Times may vary on Special Events days. 24-hour information line on 0870 600 8880 will confirm opening times and special events. Admission charge grants admission to castle and grounds for one year from date of purchase.

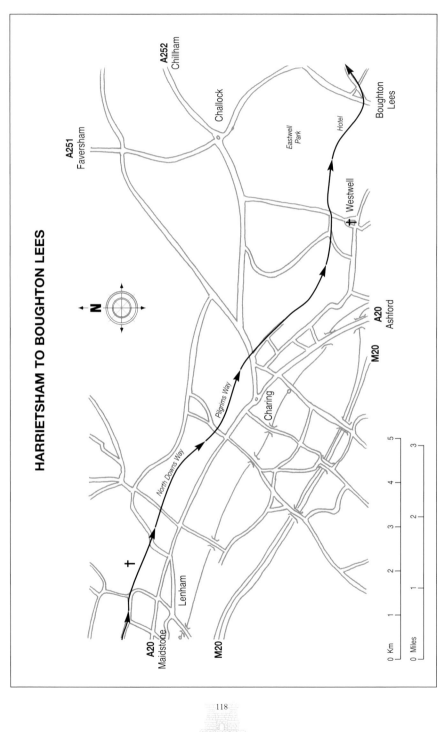

HARRIETSHAM TO BOUGHTON LEES

A251
Faversham

A252
Chillham

Challock

Eastwell
Park

Hotel

Westwell

Boughton
Lees

Pilgrims Way

North Downs Way

Charing

A20
Ashford

M20

A20
Maidstone

Lenham

M20

N

0 Km   1   2   3   4   5
0 Miles   1   2   3

Leeds Castle to Chilham

Another long section, dominated by the North Downs Way as it makes its way east above Lenham to the road at Charing Hill. Continuing south-easterly the Way proceeds through Eastwell Park, with its ruined church and large lake, to Boughton Lees, then on to the impressive church at Boughton Aluph. From here is a long, steady ascent up Soakham Down and into King's Wood, a significant wooded area along the top of the North Downs. Leaving the wood a track leads to a lane which is followed to the square at Chilham.

Route: Continue past the castle entrance to the Broomfield Gate, cutting across left at the public footpath signpost and straight across the road to the A20, which cross with care, turning right and passing under the M20 and railway bridges, before turning left signposted Greenway. As the road swings off left, turn right at the No Through Road, taking the track off left in 100 yards (91m) and keeping ahead alongside trees on left. Turn right onto a good track at the end of the field (North Downs Way). DO NOT continue ahead to the woods. Cross the road to continue ahead on Pilgrim's Way, keeping ahead along gravel track as second road turns off right to Lenham. Join another road for 100 yards (91m) before turning off left at the North Downs Way signpost, passing through a gate and along a grassy stretch under the cross on the hillside. Turn left at the road for 150 yards (137m) then right at the North Downs Way signpost, crossing straight over at the next road, then bearing left by Cobham Farm. Turn right at the next road and in 50 yards (46m) left at North Downs Way signpost. Cross the A252 at Charing Hill, turning left for a few steps before turning right at Pilgrim's Way. Keep ahead along a dirt track as the concrete road swings off left, past Arthur's Seat and along a road to the T-junction. Continue ahead across the field and alongside the wood and just before Home Farm turn right then left to continue over a stile and alongside the other side of the wood. Cross the field to continue ahead along a metalled road through Eastwell Park. (13 miles/20.9km)

EASTWELL. There is no village here, just a vast park stretching for almost 2,000 acres and the largest lake in Kent, like a mini Windermere. The church of St Mary was built mainly of chalk and was slightly damaged during the Second World War and collapsed shortly afterwards, but today is preserved

Reputed to be the tomb of Richard Plantagenet.

Church of St Mary, Eastwell.

as a ruin. Its monuments have been removed for safekeeping and sent to the Victoria and Albert Museum, but it still retains a tomb attributed to Richard Plantagenet (died 1550), natural son of Richard III who, after his father's death at Bosworth, lived incognito at Eastwell and his burial is noted in the old church registers.

The hotel in the park was rebuilt in the 1920s on the site of the original mansion which was built in the sixteenth century. Lake House, to the east of the church, has recently been recognised as an unusually large late thirteenth century stone house with an upper hall. Most of the windows are nineteenth century, although four blocked original ones still survive.

Route: At the T-junction keep ahead through the kissing gate, heading diagonally left at the marker post and crossing the drive leading to Eastwell Manor Hotel. Turn left at the road and right past the green, keeping ahead at the crossroads onto Pilgrim's Way. Turn left at the North Downs Way signpost, through a metal kissing gate to the church at Boughton Aluph. (2 miles/3.2km)

BOUGHTON ALUPH.

Boughton Aluph Church.

The church of All Saints is a very large Decorated cruciform church, mostly fourteenth century but with a chancel a hundred years older. Externally it appears more quaint than beautiful, but inside its well-proportioned arcades are light and spacious and on a transept wall is what is left of the faded wall painting over 500 years old. Some of the stained glass is fourteenth century, but the crude oak screen in the Moyle chapel is one of the oldest in England, made in the thirteenth century. The large black and white monument of the recumbent Amye Clerk, who died in 1631, has her three children kneeling at her head and feet.

Outside in the small red brick building is an open fireplace in a Tudor arch, thought to be a relic of pilgrim days and next to the church stands Boughton

Chilham Castle, built by Sir Dudley Digges to a design by Inigo Jones.

Court, mainly nineteenth century but built on a rib-vaulted undercroft belonging to the fourteenth century, when Sir Thomas de Aldon was granted licence to build a fortified house in 1339.

By the green stands the old Manor House, a long building with one stack of chimneys and a fifteenth century dovecot.

Route: Continue ahead to the road, which cross to Soakham Farm, then make the long, steady ascent of Soakham Downs from which, over to the right, the chalk crown can be seen cut into the hillside of Wye Downs. It was cut by students of Wye Agricultural College in 1902 to mark the coronation of Edward VII. At the cross-tracks turn right in the direction of the North Downs Way marker, following the track round left at fork along a stony track into King's Wood, which spreads for 3 miles (4.8km) along the top of the North Downs and in places is 2 miles (3.2km) wide. Keep to the main track as the Stour Valley Walk goes off right, turning right at the gate and sharp left opposite the oast houses. Keep ahead at road into Chilham. (4 miles/6.4km)

CHILHAM. Originally a Roman stronghold where Julius Caesar would have camped. Saxon kings strengthened the Roman fortress and a keep was begun by Bishop Odo of Bayeux which was completed by a Norman knight, Fulbert de Lucy. His daughter married Richard Fitzroy, a bastard son of King John, and their younger daughter married the Earl of Atholl who was executed for treason against Edward I. The keep is intact apart from the loss of its parapet, and Royal accounts show that the £400 spent on its construction between 1171-4 was quite modest for a keep of its size. Its plan is unique for its date as octagonal towers did not become common until the thirteenth century. Its entrance is through a forebuilding, which is in two parts: a projecting stair turret and an annexe with much thinner walls. Excavations have shown that the annexe was built on the remains of an earlier Norman hall, and the blocked archway which is still visible belonged to it. The keep does not stand on a motte and extra security is provided by the low chemise wall enclosing an oblong area around it. Chilham did not remain a royal stronghold for long, however, for King John granted it to his illegitimate son and after that it changed hands quite often.

The castle bailey was demolished in Tudor times and on its site Sir Dudley Digges built his Jacobean mansion whose hexagonal layout, designed by Inigo Jones, was probably influenced by de Lucy's keep. Only five sides of the house are built, however, the remaining three forming the courtyard, and they are in brick and sandstone, but have undergone major alterations over the centuries. During the Wars of the Roses, Chilham belonged to Lord Rees, but it reverted to the Crown in the early sixteenth century and Henry VIII granted it to Sir Thomas Cheney, Warden of the Cinque Ports.

Inside the house the old oak staircases, carved mantelpieces and plaster ceilings still remain, but the house and castle ruins are privately owned and not open to the public. The magnificent gardens, at one time modified by Capability Brown, stretch for over a mile with 1300 acres of wonderful trees, and they contain the first wisteria ever to have been planted in England.

Privately owned. Gardens open second Tuesday of the month June-October 1000-1500. Admission charge.

Chilham village is fifteenth century and is dominated by its central square with the castle at one end and the church at the other. From each corner of the square of Tudor and Jacobean houses, a lane drops away, each containing attractive historic cottages, most of which date from the seventeenth century.

St Mary's church is built of flint and dates from the fourteenth century, with some traces of an earlier building and a great deal of additions and renovations dating from the sixteenth and seventeenth centuries. The Perpendicular tower dominates the church and inside there are several notable monuments, including one in memory of Lady Mary Digges whose husband, Sir Dudley Digges, commissioned the mansion.

View of lake, Eastwell Park.

View from the stile after Boughton Aluph Church.

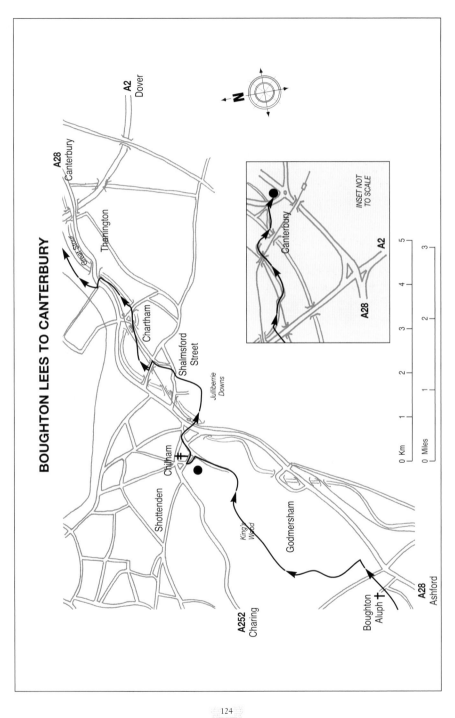

BOUGHTON LEES TO CANTERBURY

A2
Dover

A28
Canterbury

Great Stour

Thanington

Chartham

Shalmsford
Street

Julliberrie
Downs

Shottenden

Chilham

King's
Wood

Godmersham

A252
Charing

Boughton
Aluph

A28
Ashford

N

INSET NOT
TO SCALE

Canterbury

A2

A28

0 Km   1   2   3   4   5
0 Miles   1   2   3

Chilham to Canterbury

And so to the final and shortest section leading to Canterbury and journey's end. It begins by leaving Chilham by crossing the River Stour and at the same time saying farewell to the North Downs Way for the last time and following the Stour Valley Walk to Chartham. From here the route follows the river to the A28 where it becomes necessary to backtrack a little to negotiate a railway crossing before making the final approach to Canterbury by an easy, traffic free path.

Route: From the church turn left alongside the square to leave the village down The Street by Chantry House. Follow the road round right to the A28 which cross by the Stour Valley Way signpost. Over the railway and the river, crossing another part of the river from the island to the far bank where turn left by the Long Barrow of Julliberrie Downs.

JULLIBERRIE DOWNS. The Romans are said to have fought their last major battle in England here where a Neolithic long barrow is located. They certainly dug into the 4000-year-old barrow in order to bury their casualties and legend has it that the delightful name Julliberrie is derived from Julius Laberius who died in action fighting for Rome in 54BC.

Route: Follow the path ahead to join the Stour Valley Walk, turning left at the track and following the waymarkers to the crossroads, where keep ahead for 75 yards (69m) before turning off left across the field at the Stour Valley Walk signpost and turning off right half way across the field. At the road turn left at the public footpath signpost, then left over the railway bridge to continue right immediately beyond. Keep to the path alongside the railway, recrossing the railway and turning left along the road into Chartham. (3miles/4.8km)

CHARTHAM. This is the last village before Canterbury and its church of St Mary, begun at the turn of the thirteenth century, has a splendid oak roof and the oldest set of five bells in Kent. It houses some unusual brasses, one of Robert de Septvans who died in 1306 is the last military brass of the reign of Edward II. There are only three brasses older than this but none as striking as this 6 ft 3 in. long knight standing cross-legged and carrying a shield.

Route: Right out of churchyard and left along the riverside path to the bridge carrying the A28 into Canterbury. Turn left across the railway bridge then right signposted Chartham Hatch, turning right again just before the industrial units. Bear left onto the concrete track through the orchard, from where we catch the first glimpse of Canterbury cathedral ahead. Keep ahead at the cross-tracks, under the A2 then right at road. Over the level crossing then left alongside the railway, turning right at the green and left off the car park, crossing the bridge and down to the river. Pass under the ring road and follow the path to Canterbury castle. (3miles/4.8km)

CANTERBURY CASTLE. The Romans defended their city of Durovernum in the third century AD, building a wall enclosing an oval area nearly two miles in circumference and the medieval wall follows exactly the same line. More than half this circuit still survives, though there is very little Roman masonry evident, and considering the sustained level of bombing the city withstood in 1942 it is a miracle so much of medieval Canterbury survived at all.

The castle, situated just south of the roundabout by East station and at the end of Castle Street, was built shortly after the Norman invasion, around 1084, and was certainly in existence at the time of the Domesday Book. It consisted of a keep and a surrounding bailey, part of which included the Roman city walls. It was never a huge military success, for it surrendered to the French in 1216, to the Parliamentarians during the Civil War and was embarrassingly overrun by Wat Tyler's men during the Peasants' Revolt of 1381.

During the middle ages the Roman Worth Gate gave access to the castle grounds, but it was blocked up in 1548 and demolished in 1791 when Castle Street was constructed. All that remains of the castle today is the keep, which is the fifth largest in England. It was used as a prison during the reign of

Elizabeth I, but it eventually fell into disuse in 1600. An attempt was made to demolish it in the eighteenth century, but fortunately this only proceeded as far as the top floor. Last century the keep was used as a coal store for the local gasworks, but today it

Canterbury Castle. Part of its bailey included the Roman city walls. has been fully preserved.

Canterbury Castle. Built around 1084 and has the fifth largest keep in England.

When built it would have been faced with Caen stone, but much of this has since been robbed leaving only the rubble core exposed. The entrance would have been at first floor level in the north-west wall and excavations have unearthed a forebuilding.

The city wall parapet is freely accessible and the West Gate now houses a museum. To view the interior of the keep apply to the Royal Museum, High Street, Canterbury.

There is much more to explore in this wonderful city, but that, of course, is another story!

In Conclusion

Accomplishing a project of this magnitude has mixed feelings. Firstly there is the immense satisfaction of physically walking the distance, sometimes considerable distance, between one castle and another, and then exploring what we have come in search of; be it remains or substantial fortification. And then there is the anti-climax of having done what we set out to do - objective fulfilled. I think it was Mark Twain who once said: "The only thing worse than having an ambition is achieving it." So what next?

Well, let's look at what we have achieved. Richborough Castle, where all this started, is pretty impressive considering the remains are almost two thousand years old. In contrast Sandown Castle built 1500 years later is all but gone. Deal and Walmer Castles, built about the same time as Sandown, are almost as good as new and Dover Castle probably attracts more visitors than any other castle in Kent.

Now we move away from the coast to a different type of castle altogether, at Castle Hill, overlooking the new Eurotunnel Rail Terminal at the back of Folkestone. This ringwork and bailey castle is still remarkably significant considering its remains are almost a thousand years old, for it is still possible to see how its earth banks and ditches would provide the main defence to the wooden bailey within.

Although secluded and aloof, Saltwood Castle owes its place in the tragic episode in English history when it sheltered the knights who, at the king's command, murdered Thomas Becket in Canterbury cathedral. Lympne Castle also has connection with the Archdeacon of Canterbury, for it was built as his fortified residence, but Stutfall Castle immediately below Lympne was built by the Romans to protect their harbour of *Portus Lemanis* and is now in a typically sorry state thanks to landslips and neglect.

Sissinghurst Castle today is visited mainly for its gardens as is Scotney Castle, although both have long and chequered histories. The site of Brenchley Castle is nothing short of disappointing, while the immense round towers of Tonbridge Castle are as impressive as the town it once defended.

Chiddingstone village is probably more attractive than its castle, which in truth is a manor house remodelled into a castellated mansion, but nothing can detract from the magnificence of Hever Castle. This is one of the heavy-weights as far as castles in Kent is concerned, not only in appearance - for it has a truly splendid setting - but also for its place in English history.

Lullingstone Castle has a truly remarkable gateway and a most pleasant approach, and the Roman Villa just down the road is acknowledged to be one of the finest Roman sites in Britain. Eynsford, a little further on from Lullingstone, has the remains of an early Norman castle of which most of the curtain wall still exists, while Cooling Castle, Kent's most northern defensive castle, saw more civil strife than foreign intervention.

The River Medway is Kent's premier waterway so surprisingly has no fewer than three castles protecting its passage. Upnor Castle was built to protect the dockyards at Chatham and failed miserably because of a lack of firepower, Rochester Castle stands proudly at the entrance to this remarkable city, while Allington Castle stands on the site that the ancient Britons felt worth defending even before the Roman invasion.

The castle at Sutton Valence was originally built to watch over the road from Maidstone to Lympne and is one of Kent's least known castles, while just down the road is Leeds castle, one of the county's best known and best situated castles, set on an island in the middle of a huge lake.

The castle at Chilham was demolished in Tudor times and in its place a huge mansion was built. The gardens are what the visitor comes to see along with displays of birds of prey, although the village is attractive enough in its own right to warrant a visit.

And finally Canterbury, not perhaps the most significant of castles and certainly not at the top of most visitors' lists of places to see in this splendid city, but it has stood since shortly after the Norman conquest and is mentioned in the Domesday Book so does have some impact on the developing importance of the seat of Christianity in Britain. And for our walking tour of the castles of Kent it does signify journey's end.

Transport Options

The logistics involved in undertaking a venture such as this are many and varied. The most obvious is to back-pack, that is to take all the belongings you are likely to need in a haversack and carry it with you wherever you go. To fulfil the walk in one outing will take the average walker about two weeks, although there are plenty of options for stopping and starting with easy access to enable much shorter outings at a time if preferred.

Another option is to decide on the length of a day's walk and have two cars, one parked waiting at the end of the proposed walk so that your party can drive back to retrieve the other car left parked at the beginning of the day's walk. Or, if like me, you have an understanding partner, they can drop you off at the start of the day's walk, and pick you up at the pre-arranged point later in the day.

Then there is the dependence on overnight accommodation which will need to be pre-booked, in some cases possibly long before your intended walk, especially during high season. Here you will have to pre-determine the length of your day's walk well in advance and stick to it whatever the weather and be prepared for the fact that in some instances B&Bs might not be available anywhere near where you might want them to be. The Tourist Information Centres listed at the end of this section will be able to offer some help and advice on what is available and where.

Finally there is public transport, which for the most part is quite good in Kent. As a rough guide I offer the following information for each section of the walk:

Section 1: Sandwich has a rail link connecting London-Canterbury-Deal-Walmer-Dover.
Stagecoach in East Kent Route 113 Canterbury-Sandwich-Deal-St Margaret's-Dover (operates Monday-Saturday hourly)
Stagecoach in East Kent Route 84 Deal-Walmer-Kingsdown (operates Monday-Saturday hourly)
Stagecoach in East Kent Route 90 Deal-Walmer-St Margaret's-Dover-Capel-Folkestone (operates Monday-Saturday hourly; Sunday 2 hourly)

Section 2: Rail link Dover-Folkestone
Stagecoach in East Kent/Hastings Route 711 Dover-Folkestone-Hythe (operates Monday-Saturday hourly; Sunday 2 hourly)
Stagecoach in East Kent Route 17 Canterbury-Newington-Folkestone (operates Monday-Saturday hourly; Sunday 2 hourly)

Section 3: Rail Link Ashford-Hamstreet

Kent Coach Tours Route 11B Hamstreet-Warehorne-Kenardington (operates Monday-Friday hourly; Saturday every 90 minutes)

Arriva Kent & Sussex Route 297 Ashford-Woodchurch-Tenterden (operates Monday-Saturday 2 hourly; Sunday 4 journeys)

Stagecoach in East Kent/Kent Coach Tours Route 400 Ashford-Bethersden-High Halden-Tenterden (operates Monday-Saturday hourly)

Poynters Coaches Route 523 Ashford-Biddenden (operates Monday-Friday 4 journeys; Saturday 2 journeys)

Arriva Kent & Sussex Route 4/5 Maidstone-Sissinghurst-Cranbrook-Hastings (operates Monday-Saturday hourly; Sunday 4 journeys)

Section 4/5: No services

Section 6: *Rail Link* London-Tonbridge-Ashford

Section 7: No services

Section 8: Rail Link Tonbridge-Sevenoaks-Otford-Shoreham-Eynsford

Section 9: *Red Route* 416 Cobham-Shorne Ridgeway (operates Monday-Friday 4 journeys; Saturday 3 journeys)

Red Route 417 Shorne Ridgeway-Cliffe (operates Monday-Saturday 3 journeys)

Royal Mail Customer Services Route 320 Cliffe-Cooling (operates Monday-Saturday 2 journeys)

Section 10: *Royal Mail* Customer Services Route 320 Cooling-Cliffe-Rochester (operates Monday-Saturday 2 journeys)

Section 11: *Rail Link* Rochester-Aylesford-Maidstone

Arriva Medway Towns Route 155 Rochester-Borstal-Wouldham-Aylesford-Maidstone (operates Monday-Friday hourly; Saturday every 90 minutes; Sunday 2 hourly)

Section 12: *Nu-venture* Route 13 Maidstone-Leeds-Leeds Castle-Hollingbourne (operates Monday-Friday 2 hourly; Saturday 4 journeys)

Section 13: *Rail Link* Ashford-Chilham-Canterbury

Section 14: *Rail Link* London-Rochester-Canterbury

Stagecoach in East Kent Route 652 Chilham-Chartham-Canterbury (operates

Monday-Saturday hourly)
Always check with the appropriate operator before making your journey!
Traveline (public transport info) 0870 608 2 608 www.traveline.org.uk
For train information 08457 48 49 50 www.nationalrail.co.uk

Tourist Information Centres:

Deal Visitor Information Point, Deal Library, Broad Street, Deal, Kent CT14 6ER Tel: 01304 369576 Fax: 01304 380821 www.whitecliffscountry.org.uk

Dover The Old Town Gaol, Biggin, Dover, Kent CT16 1DL Tel: 01304 205108 Fax: 01304 245409 www.whitecliffscountry.org.uk

Folkestone Visitor Centre, Harbour Street, Folkestone, Kent CT20 1QN Tel: 01303 258594 Fax: 01303 247401 www.kents-garden-coast.co.uk info@discoverfolkestone.co.uk

Hythe Visitor Centre, En Route, Red Lion Square, Hythe, Kent CT21 5AZ Tel: 01303 267799 Fax: 01303 261161 www.kents-garden-coast.co.uk hvc@enroute.co.uk

Tonbridge Castle Street, Tonbridge, Kent TN9 1BG Tel: 01732 770929 Fax: 01732 770449 tonbridgecastle@tmbc.gov.uk

Sevenoaks The Library, Buckhurst Lane, Sevenoaks, Kent TN13 1LQ Tel: 01732 450305 Fax: 01732 461959 www.sevenoaks.gov.uk tic@sevenoakstown.gov.uk

Rochester 95 High Street, Rochester, Kent ME1 1LX Tel: 01634 843666 Fax: 01634 847891 www.medway.gov.uk/tourism Visitor.centre@medway.gov.uk

Maidstone Town Hall, Middle Row, High Street, Maidstone, Kent ME14 1TF Tel: 01622 602169 Fax: 01622 602519 tourism@maidstone.gov.uk www.tour-maidstone.com

Canterbury 12/14 Sun Street, Buttermarket, Canterbury, Kent CT1 2HX Tel: 01227 378100 Fax: 01227 378101 www.canterbury.co.uk canterburyinformation@canterbury.gov.uk

Bibliography

There are numerous books about all aspects of Kent, but here are some of the titles used in the preparation of this guide:

A Guide to Historic Kent, Irene Hales, Meresborough Books (1984)

The Buildings of England - North East and East Kent, John Newman, Yale University Press (2002)

The Buildings of England - West Kent and the Weald, John Newman, Yale University Press (2002)

The King's England - Kent, Arthur Mee, Hodder & Stoughton (1936)

County Companion - Kent, Hilary Arnold, Cadogan Books, London (1983)

The Pilgrims' Way in Kent, Donald Maxwell, Kent Messenger (1932)

Walking the Cathedral Cities of England, Rowland Mead, New Holland (2003)

Discovering Castles in England and Wales, John Kinross, Shire Publications Ltd (1973)

English Castles, Adrian Pettifer, The Boydell Press (1995)

Richborough Castle, J.P. Bushe-Fox, Department of the Environment (1975)

Dover Castle, R. Allen Brown, Department of the Environment (1967)

Invicta - The Story of a Royal Castle, revised in 1981 from an original text by Rev. S.W.G. Elvins

The Tunnels of Dover Castle, Roy Humphreys

Sissinghurst Castle, Nigel Nicholson, The National Trust (1964)

Scotney Castle, The National Trust (1984)

Hever Castle and Gardens, Gavin Astor (1973)

Guide to The Friars Aylesford

Leeds Castle, Nick McCann, Leeds Castle Enterprises (2002)

A Guide to the Roman Remains in Britain, Roger J.A. Wilson, Constable (2002)

And an enormous selection of church guides from all around the county, which apart from describing the buildings themselves often provide "snippets" of local history.